ADVANCE PRAISE FOR *#BLACKINSCHOOL*

"*#BlackInSchool* offers a critical perspective on anti-black racism in the education system from the people we need to hear from most on this matter—Black students. [This] is a book educators, administrators, and politicians should read and study with careful consideration and humble reflection." —JAEL RICHARDSON, author of *Gutter Child*

"*#BlackInSchool* offers a powerful 'must read' accounting of the lived experiences of Blacknesses and anti-Black racism in schools, and by extension, an indictment of society. It is a call for action from the forces of power to address the cancer of racism and anti-racist violence meted on Black bodies and the African humanity. Habiba Cooper Diallo challenges us to think through our politics to build anti-colonial solidarities with oppressed communities in these moments when we can easily be seduced by fake radicalism. We must continue to bear witness to history and the culture of race denialism that afflict our communities. Above all, we need vigilance as we tell our stories to compel action and bring true human liberation." —GEORGE J. SEFA DEI, Director, Centre for Integrative Anti-Racism Studies, University of Toronto

"Habiba Cooper Diallo's book and reflective narrative writings are vivid in their description, candid in their authenticity, and courageous in their interrogation of how the school system reinforces institutional practices regarding race, racism, and antiblackness. From the curriculum to teacher-student relations, Habiba Cooper Diallo has a lot to offer to reveal the problem of a school culture that alienates Black students. Educators' approaches to teaching Black students will be remarkably enhanced by reading about Habiba's personal experiences and narrative accounts of schooling." —DR. DOLANA MOGADIME, Professor, Faculty of Education, Brock University

#BLACK INSCHOOL

HABIBA COOPER DIALLO

FOREWORD BY AWAD IBRAHIM

 University of Regina Press

Printed and bound in Canada at Imprimerie Gauvin. The text of this book is printed on 100% post-consumer recycled paper with earth-friendly vegetable-based inks.

COVER ART: "School Lockers Ransacked Front" by alswart / Adobe Stock

COVER AND BOOK DESIGN: Duncan Campbell, University of Regina Press
COPY EDITOR: Amber Riaz
PROOFREADER: Rachel Taylor

Library and Archives Canada Cataloguing in Publication

TITLE: #BlackInSchool / Habiba Cooper Diallo ; foreword by Awad Ibrahim.

OTHER TITLES: BlackInSchool | Black in school

NAMES: Diallo, Habiba Cooper, author.

IDENTIFIERS: Canadiana (print) 2021023007X | Canadiana (ebook) 20210230355 | ISBN 9780889778184 (softcover) | ISBN 9780889778191 (hardcover) | ISBN 9780889778207 (PDF) | ISBN 9780889778214 (EPUB)

SUBJECTS: LCSH: Diallo, Habiba Cooper,—Diaries. | LCSH: High school students,—Saskatchewan,—Regina,—Diaries. | LCSH: Students, Black,—Saskatchewan,—Regina,—Diaries. | LCSH: Racism in education,—Saskatchewan,—Regina. | LCSH: Racism,—Saskatchewan,—Regina. | LCSH: High schools,—Saskatchewan,— Regina. | LCGFT: Diaries.

CLASSIFICATION: LCC LC212.3.C33 R44 2021 | DDC 370.89/96071,—dc23

10 9 8 7 6 5 4 3 2 1

University of Regina Press, University of Regina
Regina, Saskatchewan, Canada, S4S 0A2
TEL: (306) 585-4758 FAX: (306) 585-4699
U OF R PRESS   WEB: www.uofrpress.ca

We acknowledge the support of the Canada Council for the Arts for our publishing program. We acknowledge the financial support of the Government of Canada. / Nous reconnaissons l'appui financier du gouvernement du Canada. This publication was made possible with support from Creative Saskatchewan's Book Publishing Production Grant Program.

For all the Black high schoolers and students of the world.

Rise up.

CONTENTS

PART III

CONCLUSION

NARRATING THE BLACK BODY IN HIGH SCHOOLS: PUT YOUR EARS TO THE GROUND AND LISTEN!

DR. AWAD IBRAHIM

n Jostein Gaarder's bestselling novel, *Sophie's World*, the protagonist, Alberto, has a wonderful discussion about the nature of existence with fourteen-year-old Sophie. He reminds us that, as humans, "We are condemned to improvise. We are like actors dragged onto the stage without having learned our lines, with no script and no prompter to whisper stage directions to us. We must decide for ourselves how to live."[1] If this is so, then, students as well as educators are left with this existential and epistemic question: In this improvised theater that is called life (or education), which direction does one or should one take and how does one

---

1   Jostein Gaarder, *Sophie's World: A Novel about the History of Philosophy* (New York: Berkley Books, 1996), 457.

get there? This question could not be more urgent, especially if one is embodying the Black body in what might be described as a post–George Floyd moment, a moment in which the whole globe witnessed how deadly it was to embody the Black body and how gratuitous it was to murder it.

Through a bricolage of journal entries that were written while in Grades 11 and 12, *#BlackInSchool* not only answers this difficult question but does so while fearlessly staring nihilism and hopelessness in the face. Grounded in the real, *#BlackInSchool* does envision a better future, but one that is not without a cost. As a Black educator and a father, I found myself apologizing to Habiba that she had to endure so much pain at such an early age. Did we as Black adults fail our Black kids by leaving them to encounter such an ugly world? This question reminds us of the beauty as well as the difficulty of #ExistingWhileBlack (to use Habiba's term). To retain our humanity, Black people's history for a long time now has been a history of struggle from one generation to the next. If Habiba is the next generation, however, then we as Black people have pulled the ship closer to the shore of humanity. Not only are we equipping our young Black people with tools-of-struggle but also with a language that will enable them to write their own stories and spell their own names. With Habiba, we can proudly say, we are creating a "strong poet."[2]

Once in a while, someone comes in with strong conviction, clear mind, and convincing articulation to show us the way. Despite that person's age, their articulation, their ideas,

---

2   Harold Bloom, *The Anxiety of Influence: A Theory of Poetry* (New York: Oxford University Press, 1973).

and the totality of their script are so freshly new that we cannot resist reading and wrestling with them, and may even take them in as our own. This is (the power of) the strong poet. This is Habiba, a young person who has the gift of language and who dares to pursue happiness in the face of formidable difficulties. Some of these difficulties are out of her control (like the passing of her father at a very early age), but others are intentionally inflicted on her (like the many experiences of racism and epistemic violence Habiba tells in her journal entries).

As American philosopher Richard Rorty explains, the strong poets do not simply write verses.[3] They are so eloquent in their language, so visionary in their conviction that the familiar, the immediate, and the known become unfamiliar and unknown. The strong poets, Rorty adds, are horrified of simply being "a copy or a replica"; they have the courage and audacity to engage, look for, and think through the "blind impresses," the gaps and the blind spots of thoughts, ideas, and practices. The blind impresses are the difficult knowledges—problems, if you like—that society prefers not to face, be it (micro-)aggression, blatant racism, war, xenophobia, or ethno-supremacy. In the face of formidable pressure, the strong poets will choose to walk through these "problems," so to speak, and deal with them at the individual, national, and global level.

This is exactly what we get with Habiba's *#BlackInSchool*. It is worth repeating that these journals were written in

---

3   Richard Rorty, *Contingency, Irony, and Solidarity* (Cambridge: Cambridge University Press, 1989).

Grades 11 and 12. I need to remind myself of that. Making the autobiographical biographical and the personal political, *#BlackInSchool* takes language to a *whole nother level*. *#BlackInSchool* opens cracks through which we hear a voice of a young person who is grounded in the real, has a deep understanding of the world around her in a way that is beyond her age, and who knows what it means and how to become fully human. In *#BlackInSchool*, we encounter a young cultural critic and social theorist who knows not only how to tell one's own story but to theorize while doing so; a strong poet who is asking us to put our ears to the ground and listen to the kids, especially Black kids. When we do that, we will find ourselves snapping our fingers while reading these journal entries; and we will have a better understanding of what it means to be #BlackInSchool in Canada. Clearly, our best is here, within these journal entries, but our absolute best is yet to come—as students and educators, but also as human beings. Though it needs to be a collective effort, Habiba is offering us a compass in *#BlackInSchool* that will help us find our absolute best and bring it into existence. WORD!

Awad Ibrahim
University of Ottawa
June 2021

ACKNOWLEDGEMENTS

All praises be to God.

To my mother Afua, for teaching me how to carry on in spite of the pain and holding me throughout. I love you. My editor Kelley Jo Burke, for believing in my voice and enabling me to share it with the world. Awad Ibrahim, for giving me the first opportunity to express my thoughts on this topic. Aunty Fatima Cajee and Aunt Lynn, for opening your home to me when my mother was away. Isaac and El, for your remarkable support. Melinda Daye and Sean Grouse, for your advocacy. Claudine and Jason, for welcoming us when we were new. Karolyn Smardz Frost, for being a true friend to our family and for your advice during the publishing process. Paulene Harvey, for helping me see my gift again and again. Olive Philipps and Denise Allen, for making Halifax feel more like home. Sean Prpick, Bruce Walsh, and Karen Clark of University of Regina Press for wanting the world to know this story. My family. To my late father, Alpha Madiou, for taking me to school on my first day of Grade 9, nervous as I was, and wrapping me in his love always.

INTRODUCTION

You alone are enough. You have nothing to
prove to anybody. —MAYA ANGELOU

My initial goal in offering my journal from Grade 11 and 12 for publication was to shed light on my experience as a Black, female student in high school.[1]

As you will see, many of the negative experiences I had in high school were a direct result of my being Black, or African. Throughout the book, I frequently used the terms "Black" and "African" interchangeably. I am aware that such interchangeability is not always correct; nonetheless, the

....

1 As I re-read these entries at twenty-three years old, and having now completed my undergraduate studies, I am realizing that the issues that bothered me at the time remain the same due to a failure on the part of our educational system to meaningfully address them. One would think that if high school provided a non-academic skill set, it would have something to do with personal interaction or self-development. In my case, high school hardened me, and gave me tools I can now use to combat injustice for the rest of my life. That has already proven to be a good thing. Whether I should have gotten such a skill set from school is questionable; school is not the place one expects to learn to fight injustice. But for me, it was.

context of this book, and my experience in high school, legit-imize the interchangeability of the two words.

I began high school in September 2010 in Toronto, Ontario, where I completed Grade 9. My father passed away in October of that year, and the following year I found myself moving to the edge of the country when my mother took up a teaching position in Halifax, Nova Scotia. I completed the last three years of high school there. One thing that I was keenly aware of throughout my high school education and experience was my race and the micro-aggressions of racism inflicted upon the bodies of Black students. By "body" I am referring not only to the physical bodies of Black students, but also to our mental, emotional, and spiritual bodies, all of which coalesce to make us human. These micro-aggressions include, but are not limited to, verbal assaults; epistemic violence, as evidenced through some of my entries on cur-ricular racism; racial profiling by the police in schools; and teacher-student harassment. I also could not ignore the more insidious macro-aggressions; for example, the systemic in-stitutionalized racism that expresses itself in racist notions embodied by teachers, staff and administration, and in the curriculum taught to students.

Naturally, students want to do well. We all strive to do well. I strove to do well. But, as a Black student, I constant-ly found myself pushing against abrasive elements within school. In reflecting upon this key moment of my life, I give you a glimpse into a part of my journey through grief, outrage, and awakening. My father's death and my family's reloca-tion to another province took a huge toll on me emotionally, and though it was destiny, I sometimes wonder if all that I experienced in high school might not have seemed so sharp and offensive had I not been grieving.

As you read this book, I would like you to remember that, while during this period I was often sad, I was still trying my best to self-actualize and reach my goals. Some of my most cherished high school moments were trips with my friend to the ice cream shop, or to Tim Hortons in the local plaza on warm summer evenings; having her over after school and showing her dance moves in my living room; travelling together after school to the mall and chatting for hours in the mall's food court; choreographing a dance for my school's multicultural show, which required many practices with my group after school in empty classrooms, or at my home or theirs. Those moments offered comfort, joy, and clarity absent from a too often abrasive environment at school. My friend is not Black; she is of colour, and a refugee. As a result of knowing her, I was introduced to the unique challenges faced by refugee and new-immigrant children at my school, which ranged from the disdain they received from teachers, to being pressured by counsellors into classes that left them without prerequisites for post-secondary education even though they had the level of competency in English required to take the pre-university courses. While we experienced different forms of discrimination—theirs largely based on immigration and language, and mine based on race—there was a mutual feeling of not belonging. However, I spoke fluent English and had a strong sense of my rights in school.

#BlackInSchool is timely given the reality faced by Blacks in today's world. While this book deals with my

experiences as a Black youth in high school, I realize that the issues I address do not exist in a vacuum. They exist alongside horrific police brutality towards Black people; alongside frisking and street checks; along with racial profiling in Halifax, Nova Scotia, where Blacks are randomly stopped and interrogated by police six times more than people of other races.[2] Therefore, the title *#BlackInSchool* could easily be expanded to include: #TravellingWhileBlack, or #ShoppingWhileBlack, or #WalkingWhileBlack—the point being that #ExistingWhileBlack in societies that continue to not only question our humanity, but treat us as undeserving of basic human rights, is a constant in Black lives.

So despite the doubts and insecurities I have about sharing this journal with the world—written when I was very young—when reminded of the murder of Andrew Loku by Toronto police, or of the body of a slain eighteen-year-old Mike Brown lying in the street, of nineteen-year-old Renisha McBride, of Amadou Diallo shot at forty-one times in total, and with nineteen of the bullets penetrating his corpse, or even of Santina Rao, viciously attacked by police in a Halifax Walmart in front of her two babies, I become convinced that this story needs telling. My hope for this work is that it will be a useful part of the long and ongoing fight to bring an end to anti-Black racism and ultimately create a loving, respectful, and inclusive world for everyone.

The journal is presented almost entirely as it was written during my school years; I have corrected some grammar and

2   Dr. Scot Wortley, *Halifax, Nova Scotia: Street Checks Report* (NS Human Rights Commission, 2019).

vocabulary errors but only when they might get in the way of readability. Additions to the narrative that I have made as an adult, including name changes to protect the privacy of some of the people I referenced, are set inside non-standard parentheses { }. Any clarifications of fact are provided in footnotes and were made by me as an adult. Most of the quotations that open many of the chapters were chosen by me in 2019 and 2020.

Anything else is from the original journal and comprises the thoughts of a young student, going through a difficult few years, choosing not to give up, but instead, to document, process, and *resist* the constant abrasions of systemic racism as they rasped against her young body.

PART I

#BLACKINSCHOOL

AUTUMN 2012

The most common way people give up their power
is by thinking they don't have any.
—ALICE WALKER, *The Colour Purple*

I am a Black student in Canada. April 6, 2013 will mark my seventeenth birthday and my thirteenth year in school. I am becoming increasingly aware of the impact of school on the bodies of Black children in Canada.

Two years ago, in the ninth grade, I recall walking down a hallway to attend a school newspaper meeting when I was struck by what I consider to be an extremely disturbing image of Black bodies on the wall. As part of an assignment, students had posted a photograph from the 1984 Ethiopian famine. The bodies depicted were naked, dark and gaunt, and shown to be crawling. I was horrified, humiliated, and indignant all at once.

I quickly went to the school's administration to express my discontent with the photograph; it was removed from the wall the next day.

Still, I ask myself: why was I the one to bring the image to the attention of the administration? Had the students who worked on the assignment not been able to see how degrading the image was, and assess the impact it would have on Ethiopian children in the school or on other Blacks and Africans for that matter? Why had the teachers not analyzed the image? Finally—and it is shameful that I must even consider this point—as passersby, why hadn't other staff found the image problematic? And if they had, indeed, found it problematic, why had they neglected to express that sentiment?

Such experiences are commonplace for Black students. They are incessant—in elementary through high school, and beyond; that is, if we are not too discouraged to pursue higher education.

Our humanity, it seems, is continually eroded. We experience this through *Kony 2012*[3] assemblies in which we are shown videos of slaughtered Black bodies—decapitated and severed. We experience this in the classroom when all the presentations pertaining to Africa harp on the gothic features of the continent—the perpetual "tribal" warfare, famine, and disease—or when entering school in the morning and being assaulted by a student's voice: "The worst countries to live in are Uganda, Sudan, and Congo—if you walk into one of those places you'll just die."

---

3   A film whose purpose was to promote a charitable push to have Ugandan cult and militia leader, indicted war criminal, and International Criminal Court fugitive Joseph Kony arrested by the end of 2012. The film ultimately brought to the public consciousness the limits of "clicktivism" and "white saviour industrial complex" that is the foundation of so many seemingly well-meaning campaigns.

How is it that such a one-sided story of Blackness and Africa takes precedence? What does it do to one's spirit when one's humanity is constantly under attack? When the academy, intentionally or not, perpetuates the idea of her "subhumanity"? When the continent of her origin is reduced to two, or three, "high conflict" countries? And when the leaders of those countries are belittled? Most importantly, what does this do to this young Black body?

Every night on returning home from school, I turn to my diary—an outlet for the release of negative sentiments which lodge themselves in my body throughout the day—or I immerse myself in Reggae and *Wassoulou* dance as a way of recharging my spirit by connecting with one of the most intimate aspects of my personhood, my culture, something which is abrogated and denied me, as well as the masses of other Black students, in high school.

#HIGHSCHOOLANDTHEBLACKBODY
15 NOVEMBER 2012

Racism is a visceral experience . . . it dislodges brains, blocks
airways, rips muscle, extracts organs, cracks bones, breaks teeth.
You must never look away from this. You must always remember
that the sociology, the history, the economics, the graphs, the
charts, the regressions all land, with great violence, upon the body.

—TA-NEHISI COATES, *Between the World and Me*

High school hurts the Black Body. High school is hard
enough on any young body. {All students grapple with
stress, lack of sleep, lugging heavy textbooks through
icy Canadian winters, and up and down stairs, and
regular teen angst,} but there is a whole other layer of constant and in some ways unseen violence that is done to young
Black bodies in high school that needs to be recognized, because Black students must also deal with the racial stresses
involved in going to school.

During the lunch hour a student quite often remarks, and
I heard it so many times that it is sickening: "Don't waste
your food, because there are starving children in Africa who

would be grateful for it," or "There are places in the world—like Africa—where children cannot go to school, so be thankful that you're getting an education." "Africa" has become a kind of punctuation in our sentences, inserted wherever conscience and empathy is needed. Though, is the impetus for these catchphrases about Africa really empathy when students who self-identify as continental African contradict the notions of an impoverished, needy Africa?

Eventually these statements take on the form of violence—epistemic violence—rendering the acquisition of knowledge difficult for the Black student. How is one to concentrate on a chemistry lesson or a biology assignment after being told that Africans like herself cannot go to school?

High school stigmatizes the Black Body. At my school, I recently witnessed the arrest of a Black student. Prior to the incident, two officers were interrogating him and his non-Black friend on school property. The latter was escorted back inside the school, while the former was kept outside for further interrogation. I continued to watch through the window. The officer soon began to search him, clearly unable to find anything worthy of arrest. She persisted nonetheless, and in doing so provoked him, for he became frantic, kicking off his shoes and waving his arms as he proclaimed his innocence. The officer was unrelenting. Within seconds, his chest was pressed against the side of the car, his back to me, and his hands cuffed. Adding insult to injury, a student adjacent to me, having also witnessed the arrest, remarked, "He knows the drill."

I could feel my heart sink, and soon the tears began to flow—a physical manifestation of the impact of high school on the Black Body—as he was driven away, coerced away, from an education, from the school that, we are told, is the most essential component of a student's success in the future. We are told that school is a "safe" and "healthy" place. Given all that, how can it coexist with legal, police-authorized coercion away from learning?

High school hinders the Black Body. The bell rang exactly nine minutes after the arrest. Shattered and demoralized as I was, I still had to report to my fourth-period biology class. I had to fulfill my academic responsibility.

High school nullifies the Black Body. In spite of the major contributions Blacks have made and continue to make to Canadian society, and more obviously our sheer presence in the country, in school, there is an erasure of the histories and contemporary experiences of Blacks in Canada. During Remembrance Day ceremonies, why don't we remember the Black veterans of World War I from Nova Scotia's No. 2 Construction Battalion? I often look through my textbooks—history, chemistry, and biology, just to name a few—and count the bodies depicted as inventors, prominent political figures, and theoreticians relative to those who are victims of war, inadequate health care, famine, and political instability. The former are usually images of white bodies, while the latter people of colour—typically Blacks.

How does the erasure of the Black experience and ultimately the suppression of Black students nullify the Black Body? The first strike is psychological—Black students' consciousness of the lack of recognition for the Black experience. This is followed by an emotional response—dejection and apathy towards school, as there is no relevance to the experience for Black students as human beings. Finally, the Black student goes into a state of corporeal shock, questioning the significance of her skin, her features, her hair, and fundamentally her body, in a system that suppresses the expression of her humanity.

#TOBEABLACKSTUDENT

I FEBRUARY 2013

> Many Africans succumb to the idea that they can't do things
> because of what society says. Images of Africa are negative—
> war, corruption, poverty. We need to be proud of our culture.
>
> —DAMBISA MOYO, interview, *New Statesman*

My time in school has been enlightening and intellectually stimulating. For literary assignments, I have had the pleasure of reading Shakespeare's *Romeo and Juliet* and Michael Ondaatje's *In the Skin of a Lion*. I have had the opportunity to listen to Alexandre Trudeau and Michael Ignatieff at school assemblies. I have written about the accomplishments of French microbiologist Louis Pasteur, and the military expeditions of Napoleon Bonaparte. However, my experience in school continues to be an emotional and spiritual struggle.

My mother can attest. She is the one who is often made to absorb the consequences of this struggle—my tears of indignation upon returning home from an assembly at which a representative from a non-governmental organization (NGO) working in "high conflict" regions labels Black children as poverty-stricken and needy, or my frequent articulation of dampened morale, psychic apathy, and corporeal fatigue.

My Black peers share the same sentiments—high school is a collective struggle for Black students. When we come together at each other's homes, at the mall, at the movies, or while attending conferences on Black students' education, we discuss the challenges we face in school, and offer one another words of moral support and encouragement. Such creative outlets, meetings, and discussions are forms of individual and collective catharsis. They are imperative for the sustenance of the Black Body in high school, yet time consuming as well. They take hours and days (in the case of conferences) that should go towards fulfilling academic responsibilities, completing homework, studying for tests, or doing research projects.

In November 2012, I attended a three-day conference for Black students that was geared towards providing us with tools on coping with racism in school and letting us know about career pathways and scholarships of which we would be otherwise unaware. Unsurprisingly, we all had stories to share about our encounters with white supremacy and racism in school. It was a transformative experience, however saddening. For three days, we had to divorce ourselves from the "mainstream," the "white" high school experience, in order to have such discourse. Notwithstanding the inextricable commonalities between the day-to-day lives of Black and white students, as Blacks, our lives are still marginalized. Today, although the majority of Black students in Canadian high schools are Canadian-born and so spend the same time in the Canadian educational system as our white peers—we are seen as others.

My two older siblings have also been through high school, up to eighteen years earlier than me. Their struggles have not been any different from my own, or—using my own gaze— those of my Black peers.

"THAT ENGLISH CLASS WAS F*CKED!"
23 APRIL 2013

That's the problem. We let people say stuff, and they say
it so much that it becomes okay to them and normal for us.
What's the point of having a voice if you're gonna be silent
in those moments you shouldn't be?

—ANGIE THOMAS, *The Hate U Give*

get it. I get why Black students drop out. It's the sheer
violence we're subjected to every day. I was just in the
school washroom and I overheard someone in the stall
next to me:

"That English class was f*cked! She always goes on a tangent about Black people. I know racism exists, but there are other things to do."

I interrupted and told her that maybe she should take a minute and listen to her teacher's tangents, because for someone like myself who experiences racism every day of my life at school and outside, more than going off on a "tangent" in English class is necessary to even begin talking about racism.

She simply stared at me and listened without saying anything. I'm happy I said something, for I think it made her reflect.

Oh my god, I feel like a knife has pierced my abdomen—sickening. #HighSchoolAndTheBlackBody. The chilling thing is that every school day has the potential to be like this. It is one thing to challenge these forms of constant, mundane discrimination but in the end, they can have huge emotional repercussions.

THE WORST COUNTRIES TO LIVE IN ARE UGANDA, SUDAN, AND CONGO...

25 APRIL 2013

> I write . . . for those who do not have a voice because
> they were so terrified, because we are taught to respect
> fear more than ourselves. We've been taught that silence
> would save us, but it won't. —AUDRE LORDE

started Grade 11 on September 5, 2013. It would be my first year as an International Baccalaureate (IB) diploma student.

That same month, I was introduced to the school's global philanthropic spirit with a *Kony 2012* assembly. *Oh lord,* I thought to myself sitting in the auditorium, *here we go again, Africa the hashtag inserted like a piece of punctuation wherever empathy is concerned.* In this case, it was a school-wide assembly in support of the Invisible Children organization, held after we were all shown footage from a horrific short documentary film about the tyranny of the African warlord and his regiments of child soldiers. My friend sat next to me crying.

Habiba in her high school stairwell, start of Grade 12, September 2013. Photo courtesy of the author.

I sat next to her shaking my head. "It's so sad," she whispered. "This is ridiculous," I responded, "They always love to portray Africans in this way," referring to the decapitated and severed Black bodies that saturated the film.

After the screening, one of the organization's representatives came on stage followed by a man who claimed to have been a child soldier himself and who had benefitted from the work of Invisible Children.[4] Of course, bringing him to the stage to discuss his experience would make it difficult for any student in the audience to debate the *Kony 2012* issue altogether. He was their ambassador. I would have just seemed uncouth and unsympathetic had I expressed my thoughts on the matter. I kept them to myself (with the exception of my friend). Still, I was upset.

It did not end there. I was tired of seeing Black bodies and the diverse experiences of Black people (yes, even in a "war zone" there are diverse experiences) portrayed in such a degrading and uniform manner. I quickly booked a meeting with one of the vice principals to address the issue I had with the assembly. I could feel my cheeks get hot as we discussed. She was defensive. She told me that I just got to the school and that before I criticized their actions I should learn about the school's philanthropy, such as their support for the local Gambian association. *Hah!* I laughed to myself, *as if supporting the local Gambian association has anything to do with my complaint.* Why should I learn about the other philanthropic work first? I came to discuss the *Kony 2012* assembly not the Gambian Association or Head for the Cure. *Kony 2012* was the introduction I was given. She also informed me that I was not

---

4   I, by no means, intend to mock the man's experience, for it may indeed have been true. Nonetheless, I regard the issue with due skepticism given the inconsistency in media reports and the various attestations of fiscal mismanagement on the part of the organization.

the only student who was upset by the assembly. Apparently, two boys who were also from that region (Uganda, Sudan) went to her and said, "It's not all like that. That has not been our experience, so we did not appreciate how our homeland was portrayed by the film." From our discussion, I learned that the school had not previewed the film. The organization had simply approached the school about doing the assembly and they agreed without previewing the content of what they wanted to present.

A few mornings later, as I was walking into the school, I overheard two boys in front of me discussing the then-recent assembly. "The worst countries to live in are Uganda, Sudan, and Congo—if you walk into one of those places you'll just die," one of the boys said high-handedly. I think I did a double-take. I walked to them quickly and said, "You said the worst countries to live in are Uganda, Sudan, and Congo? How can you be so sure of that?"

I was being too nice. Asinine comments like that don't even deserve to be entertained. My question made them feel important. I ostensibly gave them the opportunity to "educate" me as to why those countries are so horrible to live in. A quick side note: it just occurred to me how moronic his statement really was. How could you live in a country if, upon "walking into" that country, you die? That doesn't make sense. The possibility to *live* in the country would not exist—you would die before getting to live in it. A long debate ensued: I, insisting that they take into account the entirety of the reasons for which they deemed those countries so horrible—war, poverty, etc. They, staunchly defending their premise.

They dismissed all that I was saying; they knew the *truth* about Africa because they watched TV channels like CNN and BBC. They would not back down. I was not about to either. I saw Ms. J., our student support worker, hovering in the area, a concerned expression on her face as she watched our debate. She eventually disappeared. I decided that I should probably head on up to my first-period biology class. I was already late. I could tell that the boys were in for the win; I just wanted them to reconsider their arguments . . . *entirely*. I closed off by telling them to consider opposing viewpoints to the arguments they put forth, that it's critical they analyze their points from a holistic perspective.

As I made my way upstairs, I could feel my body grow heavy. I was hit by a sudden wave of melancholy. I dragged myself into the girl's washroom, perched on the countertop and dug around in my bag for my phone.

"Mom," I croaked into the receiver.

"What's going on? Why are you crying?!"

I told her about the argument with the boys.

"Okay, stay right there. I'm coming. I'm coming now. I've had enough of this. Do you have class now?"

"Yes."

"Is there somewhere you could go to cool off?" I told her I could go to Ms. J.'s.

"Okay, go there. I will see you soon."

"What happened?!" Ms. J. exclaimed as I got in. "I saw you down there talking to those boys. I wasn't sure if I should have stayed, but you looked really upset." I gave her a recap, telling her that I was particularly bothered by how fierce they were in asserting their one-sided, distorted statements about Africa. I felt assaulted. "You should have gotten their names," she said.

"I wasn't even thinking to do that."

"Well yes, because that's something that should be taken up with the principal."

I cried, telling her about the experience I was having at the school, the constant micro-aggressions associated with African-ness and the sheer racism that was so deeply embedded in the school culture.

"You need to assert your Canadian identity," she told me. "You were born here. You too are Canadian."

"Yes," I responded, "but Africa is a part of me too. I am half African."

"Who is from Africa for you?" She brought out a map, and I pointed to where in Africa my father came from. The western coast, Guinea, Liberia . . . "You cannot let things like this bother you. You are bigger than that. These issues will drain you if you always take them on."

My mother arrived and demanded to see the principal. We had a follow-up discussion during which he informed us that that morning he had to educate his ten-year-old son about how there is more to Africa than malaria.

All in all, the assembly was intended to generate empathy on the part of the students for the *Kony 2012* cause. Instead, it generated this: "The worst countries to live in are Uganda, Sudan, and Congo—if you walk into one of those places you'll just die."

#ONRACISMAGAIN
30 APRIL 2013

I felt anxiety, shock . . . but also felt an urgency to act.
—MICHAËLLE JEAN, former governor general of Canada

They cannot engage any reality outside of their own:

That English class was f*cked; she's always going on a tangent about
Black people . . .

Shocked to the core.

Antigone and Shakespeare are tangents about white people.
Every day in school is a tangent about Whites—from chemistry to English. From Mendel to Frost. Praises of Coco Chanel
et la France Romantique. How about Oumou Sy or *le Sénégal*
Magnifique?

We don't have the tools.

{Anti-racist} need for information to be set against a back-
drop and Anti-sexist methodologies Contextualized.

—

"Multicultural & diverse" in name and ethnic make-up only.

The challenge isn't each individual student, but rather the systemic-ness of it.

A system in which the thoughts, and racial prejudices of each individual student are entangled.

Constant, every day, micro-accumulation.

Shocked to the system.—

Pierced with a knife.

That English class was f*cked, she said . . .

PART II

PON DI DANCEHALL
22 NOVEMBER 2013

The dance is strong magic. The body can fly without wings.
It can sing without voice. The dance is strong magic.
The dance is life.

—PEARL PRIMUS, "African Dance"

onight was my school's multicultural show. There were several acts—Dancehall, Hiplife, Persian dance, etc. Our school is the most diverse school east of Montreal. During one of our Dancehall rehearsals—led by my friend—a white girl who was considering participating in our dance entered the drama room (our practising space) and said, "Ooh, it's so sexual."

"Umm, no it's not," I bit back. "For us it's a dance."

"Yeah, it's not sexual. This is the culture," our choreographer chimed in.

Why doesn't she just leave . . . ?

She did eventually leave. Following the performance:

"Oooh Mahama, I saw you getting down and dirty," one boy told my co-dancer in reference to a Hiplife dance I choreographed. I scowled at him. *Down and dirty?* I thought. *You mean I put in all these gruelling hours to choreograph, teach, and embellish our routine (only) to be told we were getting down and dirty?*

#HypersexualizationOfTheBlackBody

Nonetheless, there was enough positive feedback to offset the Down and Dirty. One of my friends rushed me at school the next day exclaiming, "My mom loved your dance! She kept saying 'Oh my God they're so good!'" A teacher ran into me in the hallway and said, "You're the dancer, aren't you? You were glorious on stage, just glorious."

#Micro-aggressionsAndTheBlackBody

#EQUATORPEOPLE

5 DECEMBER 2013

Everyone should be afforded the opportunity to receive the education they want, but more importantly, the education they have the right to receive. —MEGHAN MARKLE

I am feeling quite disturbed at the moment.

I just finished my C-block biology class in which we learned about genetics and genetic diversity among humans.

I had a revelation. I've been having many of these lately . . . constantly actually . . . daily . . . *oh lalalaa.* They are not the most pleasant. However, they are enlightening—painfully so.

Some background for this entry:

A few classes ago my biology teacher discussed genetic mutations and the reasons why "Whites are white." I found her explanation quite racist. She said that originally, or when man first evolved, he had dark skin—my kind of skin. Over time, he got light, in other words white, and that's why today "we" (who is *we*?) have lighter, or "whiter," skin.

In saying that, she fundamentally excluded me and the darker skinned students from the "we" and ignored the existence of the Black race and other dark-skinned people.

Back to today:

She says man got lighter as he moved away from the equator—she couldn't have said from Africa?—lighter complexions were more beneficial to man as he migrated north, given the cold climate he encountered there, while darker complexions were more beneficial to "equator people" (PS: "equator people" is her terminology precisely). Nice, and there's some truth in that explanation. But, honestly, that's too simple for me.

I asked her why then do we have some dark "equator people"—and I gave the example of Australian Aboriginal people—some of whom have blue eyes and blonde hair (phenotypic features that are typically found in white populations). She seemed to get rather defensive in responding to this one. I sensed a tinge of annoyance in her tone, and her usual agitated disposition was even more unsettled.

Part 1 of her response: The Australians were colonized, therefore a lot of genetic mixing occurred, hence the blue eyes and blonde hair among some Indigenous Australians. Part 2: Furthermore, we are a global and moving people. Over time, gene pools interact which allow for atypical features among certain populations.

WHAT?!

There's so much wrong with that response. Where do I start? One, colonization of Australia has nothing to do with Aboriginal Australians having blue eyes or blonde hair. Such characteristics were identifiable in that population prior to the advent of European colonization. Hence, part 1 of her response is ahistorical and scientifically inaccurate.

According to an article in the *New York Times*, "the Aborigines are thus direct descendants of the first modern humans to leave Africa, without any genetic mixture from other races so far as can be seen at present. Their dark skin reflects an African origin and a migration and residence in latitudes near the equator, unlike Europeans and Asians whose ancestors gained the paler skin necessary for living in northern latitudes."[5]

Part 2 of her response is painfully simplistic to counter. How do you explain groups like the San of South Africa—Black African peoples who typically have light skin? Clearly, and as modern science continues to confirm, there was and is genetic and phenotypic diversity in these "equator populations" prior to large exodii out of these regions, and prior to colonization. As well, she kept referring to the "equator." Could she not have said Africa? The issue with her terminology of choice is that it's vague—I can name many light-skinned "equator peoples" (the equator passes through thirteen countries: Ecuador, Colombia, Brazil, São Tomé and Príncipe, Gabon, Republic of the Congo, Democratic Republic of the Congo, Uganda, Kenya, Somalia, Maldives, Indonesia, and Kiribati) which ultimately renders her thesis fallacious.

At the beginning of this entry, I said I was feeling quite disturbed. Here's why: my biology teacher is there to "teach" us. She is the one who marks my biology papers . . . gives me a term

---

5   Nicholas Wade, "Australian Aboriginal Hair Tells a Story of Human Migration," *New York Times*, 2011.

mark. More crucially, she's the one who disseminates information, not only to me but to my twenty-eight or so classmates. Beyond our class, she has other biology classes. Beyond these classes, she has numerous past students who are currently in university or beyond. In addition to all of that, she will get other batches of biology students in the coming years. She has taught or will "teach" so many students—dark-skinned students included—"genetics," and why "we" have lighter skin. And what she has been and will really teach is racism. If one of those students makes the awful mistake of asking my kind of question, she will employ the faulty rationale of colonialism and "equator people." I find this chilling. When you're teaching something like genetics you must be racially aware in the same way that a history teacher or a social studies teacher must be. As far as I'm concerned, all teachers should be racially aware and should have the tools and terminologies to discuss race with their students. Her explanation is just another indicator of her white privilege and her ability to continually get away with imposing it upon her students, and in my case, to offend her students.[6]

---

6   I must say here that I really liked my biology teacher as a person. She was quite nice to us, and in case she happens to read this journal, I must make it known that I find biology fascinating as a discipline and did thoroughly enjoy most of her lessons. Nonetheless, I was obviously frustrated during lessons on genetics. Our society is already divided along racial lines, yet as humanity we have so much in common politically, socially, and culturally. Indeed, genetics are important, for they determine phenotype and phenotype in turn has real-world implications: what products to use for certain hair textures, the effects of sun exposure on different complexions, etc. I feel many of our lessons were a missed opportunity to explore our commonalities. Ultimately, these lessons could have been taught in a transformative way for everyone in the class.

BOUNA TRAORE AND ZYED BENNA: #MORTSPOURRIEN

9 DECEMBER 2013

> Black boys became criminalized. So I was in constant
> dread for their lives, because they were targets
> everywhere. They still are. —TONI MORRISON, *Toni
> Morrison: The Last Interview and Other Conversations*

Today I gave a presentation to my higher-level French class . . . Our topic had to relate to the Francophonie, or the French-speaking world. I chose to shed light upon a pressing issue known to many racialized, and particularly Black, communities across the world: racial profiling by the police. I spoke about Bouna and Zyed.

Bouna and Zyed were two young French boys of Malian and Algerian descent who lived in the city of Clichy-sous-Bois, also known as the "youngest" city in France given that many of its residents are under twenty years old. However, Clichy is also known for being one of the most marginalized cities in France. On October 27, 2005, Bouna and Zyed were electrocuted on a transformer (those big electric boxes you would find in an industrial plant, or on the street outside of homes, schools, or businesses). The two young men had been (wrongfully) accused of a break-in and were being chased by police. They ran into the transformer where they hid for twenty minutes before being electrocuted as they tried to escape. The two police officers who had terrorized and intimidated them, effectively causing them to seek refuge inside the transformer, did nothing to warn them of the danger they were in or to rescue them. #StopPoliceViolence

They left them to their deaths. #AfricanLivesMatter

The communities of the French suburbs, made up of predominantly racialized people, were outraged. The residents rioted, burning ten thousand cars and thirty thousand garbage bins. They took to the streets to protest racial profiling and police brutality in their communities which ravaged the lives of many innocent youth like Bouna and Zyed. Prime Minister Dominique de Villepin declared a state of emergency in France for the first time since the War of Algeria. In February 2007, the officers were charged with "failure to assist a person in danger." Now, eight years after 2005 (the year Bouna and Zyed were electrocuted) the case remains unsettled. Their families are still awaiting some form of justice.

I was deeply affected by the story of these two young boys, by the way in which they died, that they were so young (fifteen and seventeen years old), and that the same kind of realities exist here in Canada for marginalized communities. I make it a point of duty to present on topics about the lives of people from racialized and marginalized backgrounds—people like myself. When my peers hear *Francophonie*, they automatically assume "white," that the French-speaking world—arts, culture, and society—only pertains to white people and those of European descent.

Through my presentations, I try to correct that notion. The majority of the *Francophonie* is in Africa.

I was nine years old in 2005 when Bouna and Zyed were electrocuted and the riots in the French *banlieues* (suburbs) broke out. However, it was only when I revisited the story at seventeen years old that I understood the full tragedy of it.

I made a slideshow for the presentation, which included a song on which several French singers from racialized communities collaborated as a tribute to the two boys. I guess you could say my presentation was well received. My teacher loved it, and she really appreciated the perspective I brought. My classmates did not ask many questions, but they were attentive. I realize that the topics I present are very new to them. They do not speak to most of their realities, and as such, they are not able, or not willing, to engage with them.

Not that the topics they present speak to my reality; yet, somehow, I am able to engage.

#Anyways

I concluded by telling them that the tragic deaths of Bouna and Zyed reveal the violence and social discrimination experienced by the inhabitants of Clichy-sous-Bois and other French *banlieues*, and that we cannot be passive about these issues. I told them that as International Baccalaureate (IB) students we must demand justice.

#JusticeForBounaAndZyed *#MortsPourRien*

"LIGHT PEOPLE CANNOT SURVIVE IN AFRICA" #BIOLOGYCLASS

16 DECEMBER 2013

There is no change without conviction and no purpose without empathy. —QUENTIN VERCETTY, Artist and Storyteller

In today's class, a white female student asked our teacher why darker skin tones and curlier hair are phenotypically dominant to lighter skin tones and straighter hair. She used the example of herself having a child with one of the Black male students in the class.

"If Malik and I have a baby, the baby would look like Malik. The baby's skin colour and hair texture would be closer to his than mine. Why is that?" she asked. Our teacher began by addressing the first aspect of her question: hair texture. "You have wavy hair, Leanne, and Malik's hair is what?" the teacher asked, turning to the whole class for a response.

"Curly," I chimed in, feeling very annoyed along with about three other students. *No duh teacher. You've been teaching him biology since Grade 10, you see him practically every day and you cannot describe his hair texture! He wears his hair in a large afro for heaven's sake.*

"You'll never find a Black baby with straight hair?" Leanne asked.

"I wouldn't say 'never' because it does happen sometimes, but it's not likely."

Our teacher proceeded to describe the bell curve distribution of traits and polygenic inheritance to describe the second aspect of Leanne's question: skin colour. She kept using the expression "middle-of-the-road skin tone." *Geeesh*. That super-annoyed me. Whatever does "middle-of-the-road skin tone" mean? Like asphalt with a yellow line across it, I guess.

Similar to her "equator people" lesson two weeks ago, she continued, "Man evolved in Africa near the equator . . . where they needed dark pigment . . . as time progressed mutations occurred producing recessive forms . . . light people cannot survive in Africa . . . they would have died from sunburn or skin cancer. Light-skinned people in Africa migrated later to the north (Europe) following mutations . . . our genes have not changed in ten thousand years."

I thought of my light-skinned, indigenous African cousins and I cringed. *What would their reaction be if I told them they could not survive in Africa? Well, they seem to be surviving all right . . . I think they would laugh.* I contradicted her explanation with the example of the light-skinned Kalahari people of southern Africa who are indigenous African peoples and who did not migrate from the "north" as she describes.

And I left it at that. Can she please reassess her knowledge? She's doing a huge disservice to her students while compromising the integrity of the program.

#BIOLOGYCLASSAGAIN
9 JANUARY 2014

Education is the most powerful weapon
which you can use to change the world.

—NELSON MANDELA

"Sickle cell has primarily been isolated to the continent of Africa, and the descendants of Africa." #CringingIn BiologyClass. It's the word *isolated* that got me. It sounds as if Africa and her descendants are quarantined on Sickle Cell Island.

#GUIDANCE

You must never be fearful about
what you are doing when it's right.

—ROSA PARKS

was on the bus on my way to school this morning when I began reading the front-page article of *Metro News*. A Black man was wrongfully convicted of raping a white girl some years ago. The police did a shoddy investigation . . . The case was re-opened and he was proven innocent—the plaintiff admitted that she had lied. Post-racial world? What a farce. Forty years later, and *now* the province wants to apologize? His employment prospects marred, his reputation damaged. That is, his survival is on the line.[7]

---

7   Reading such newspaper articles on my way to school was telling, for it highlighted the reality that the racism we experience in high school as Black students is not disconnected from the prejudice experienced by Black people in the wider world—be it at work, at the airport, or, in the case of this man, in the criminal justice system.

Anyway, I moseyed on into school and went straight to the guidance office. We'd had two consecutive snow days[8] so I had missed my 8:50 a.m. guidance appointment that had been scheduled for the day before. At 8:37 a.m. the receptionist told me that my counsellor was not in yet, and that I could go put my belongings in my locker and come back down. Around 8:50 a.m. my counsellor was heading towards the office.

Before she even greeted me (well, she never greeted me at all), she hurriedly told me "Oh, we're going to have to re-schedule your appointment to tomorrow." The only logical thought that came to my mind was *Why?*

"It's very brief," I said coolly. "It's just a matter of you adding your signature."

"I can do that out here, then," she responded, meaning in the main area as opposed to in her office.

"Okay."

She then proceeded to check her appointment schedule on the receptionist's computer. "Are you Mona?" she asked the student sitting across from me. Indeed, she was Mona. To me she reiterated what she said earlier about having to reschedule. She could have used the amount of time and energy she put into resisting signing my forms to quickly sign them and I would have been out within five minutes of her arrival.

"April 1 is soon," I say.

"Oh, that means you left it till late."

---

8   A day on which school is closed due to heavy snowfall or extreme winter weather.

Whether I left it till late is not the point. Tomorrow is a weekend, and I intend to mail the scholarship forms then. The deadlines are actually in late April and May, but I know guidance at my school—you'd be lucky to get an appointment in two weeks' time. Appointment wait times are a month on average. There are three counsellors for a student population of about fifteen hundred—ridiculous.

Finally, she signed one of my forms. For the second one she was concerned about whether it was one of those scholarships that allows only one nominee per school. I assured her that it wasn't, but even if it were, so what? I didn't have time this morning, but I'm going to ask her about that later today, when I go to retrieve the form from her. She told me to come back at the end of the day. The end of the day is definitely better than sometime in late April.

I'm honestly not a fan of the administrative processes at most institutions. They are not in place to benefit the student.

#MyFrustrationsAreSometimesJustFrustrations

"I SAID IT IS MY BUSINESS *DEH*"
21 MARCH 2014

Any acceptance of humiliation, indignity,
or insult is acceptance of inferiority.

—WINNIE MADIKIZELA-MANDELA

walked into school this morning and there were posters all over the walls advertising a six-kilometre walk to raise awareness about women and children who carry water on their backs. The idea is for the participants to walk six kilometres with one litre of water on their backs in solidarity with those who do.

I asked two fellow classmates—student government people—if they knew who was behind the event. As it turned out, they were the organizers. I asked them right then and there: "What's your purpose for doing this?"

"To raise awareness about the 'issue.'"

"Raise awareness and then what?"

"It'll help to raise money for organizations that will build wells closer to the people's homes."

"It's ridiculous."

"It's better than people being ignorant about what's going on."

As I got in the elevator to head up to my first-period biology class, a teacher (already in the elevator) asked me, "Why do you take the elevator?" I could sense the harassment brewing. #TheStoryOfMyLifeInTheElevator

Me: Because I have an elevator pass.

Teacher: Why?

Me: I don't want to tell you.

Teacher: You know, that's not a very respectful way to respond.

Me: I have an elevator pass because I spoke with my vice principal, and that's my business.

Teacher: So, a better question to ask would be: where is your elevator pass?

Me: I don't have it on me.

Teacher: Now, that's a problem.

Me: No, I think you want to start creating problems, and I'm feeling very frustrated right now so I'm not going to engage.

I walk out of the elevator.

All within the first fifteen minutes of school . . . #High SchoolAndTheBlackBody

ON POSTERS IN SCHOOL
25 MARCH 2014

Canada is a country that is selective in the
history it chooses to highlight and celebrate.
—AMANDA PARRIS, CBC Radio host, broadcaster

There is a graphic whitewashing of school through posters. In classes, images of Einstein, scenes from *Hamlet*, *Pride and Prejudice*, etc., are plastered to walls. Every so often, you catch a glimpse of the token Black "messiah-fied"—as my friend would say—through the Black History Month posters produced every year.

I am not necessarily opposed to these posters, as they do highlight the important contributions of Black Canadians to Canadian society—something that is always ignored by mainstream media and literature. My mother is actually featured on one of the posters, which is in my school's library, for her ground-breaking work on slavery in Canada. The problem, however, is that when contrasted to the "white" posters, it becomes obvious that Blackness in

Canada is "messiah-fied" at best, "stigmatized" and "nullified" at worst, but never "normal."

The posters do bring Blackness to the attention of students and staff in a celebratory way. Every Black History Month you can count on a poster highlighting Black achievement, accompanied by a traditional African dance put on by the students, or an assembly featuring a prominent Black figure who tells students, "I did it in spite of racism, and so can you!" While all this is great, it does not critically engage the day-to-day reality of Black students in an educational system that nullifies our lived experiences.

For example, I am aware—have been aware since elementary school—that Rosa Parks was the catalyst for the Montgomery bus boycott, that Dr. Martin Luther King gave the foundational "I have a dream" speech. Thanks to anti-racist, Civil Rights activists like Parks and Dr. King, Blacks have made several social gains with regards to inclusion of Blacks in education and in other aspects of society. Now, how can we use their legacies to challenge the racist, anti-Black realities of today that alienate Black students in high school?

In addition to the African dance performance, another option could be to have a course or a section in the history curriculum that includes an analysis of the nuances of African dance forms—Sabar, Eskista, Coupé Decalé, Soukous, Ndombolo, Mandiani, Kwela—and talks by experts about how many of these genres were used as a form of resistance against imperialist rule (as in the case of South African Kwela).

Still, the Black History Month posters are fantastic. Nonetheless, time and time again, their relevance has been questioned.

And most importantly, such inclusion for Blacks is not reflected in a critical academic fashion or in the overall context of school culture. I define school culture as the overarching spirit of the school, which is expressed through important ceremonies and events such as Remembrance Day and spirit rallies. But also, I define it as the attitudes and politics of staff and students that pervade learning and existence within the school. Certain attitudes and politics take precedence. The ones that do take precedence inevitably shape the extent to which a student feels that she belongs in the school. In my high school experience as a Black student, my ideologies about school culture have not been particularly endorsed.

I would rather that my identity as a Black student not be tokenized through "Multicultural Week." *Like, really? Only a week for multiculturalism?* I am "multicultural" (as some like to put it) all year. I do not start being multicultural at the beginning of a week in November and stop at the end of that week and then re-assimilate into Eurocentric school culture.

A WALK FOR WATER
#COGNITIVEDISSONANCE

SPRING 2014

Nothing is more terrible

than ignorance in action.

—GOETHE, *Maxims and Reflections*

Recently (as I wrote in the previous entry), student government put up posters all around the school to advertise a "Walk for Water" in order to raise "awareness" about people in the "Third World" who carry heavy loads of water on their backs. Participants of the "Walk for Water" will walk six kilometres with one litre of water on their backs to raise "awareness" and funds for the impoverished water carriers of the Third World. I think that is the most absurd and asinine idea I've heard in my life.

I approached the event organizers to express my discontent with "Walk for Water" and the fashion in which they chose to promote it. I told them frankly that I thought the idea was ridiculous, inherently flawed, and that I would never participate in such a thing. A few conceptual questions they clearly did not consider: What is the purpose of the walk? Ah yes, "awareness" as they say, but why? What is the purpose of the awareness? Isn't the proposed sympathy a little hypocritical? I told them I do not carry a backpack for the precise reason they are holding the event. Instead, when my academic load is heavy, I take a small-wheeled backpack to school. Why not do a "Walk for the students of W.H. High School?" Six kilometres with ten pounds of books on your back to raise awareness about our physiological reality as students: strained backs, poor posture, weakened muscles . . . the whole package. But of course, such a walk will not happen for the students of W.H. High School, because it's always easier, it's always sexier, and more morally expedient to make large shows of sympathy for the impoverished water carriers of the Third World, than for those who are suffering in your own school. #CognitiveDissonance. {Really! One litre of water is not even that heavy to carry!}

At least for this one of their many works of charity, they did not explicitly say "For the impoverished water carriers of Africa," but they might as well have because the poster image speaks *volumes*: it features a blue map of the African continent adjacent to *small* black footprints, supposedly representing the African people who have to walk for water. Oh, here they go again: Africa, the hashtag, inserted like a punctuation mark wherever empathy is needed. I consider such imagery of Africans to be an act of cultural violence against students who self-identify as African and who do not perpetuate a one-sided, poverty narrative of the continent. My mother had a very interesting analysis of the poster. "They've reduced the people of the continent to two small footprints. Where is the rest of the body? It's a dehumanizing portrayal," she remarked.

I showed the poster to many of my African friends to see how they would react. They were all disgusted. One lamented, "They always show Africa as being poor and dry, when not everywhere is like that." At lunch that day I had a discussion with two other African friends about how poverty is measured.

"But wouldn't you say that most people in Africa are poor?" one put forth.

"Hmmm. No. That's really hard to say," said another, who had spent her childhood in the continent. "In cities for example it's often more difficult for people to access everyday necessities such as food and water because they might not be able to afford them; whereas, in many rural areas people are self-sufficient through farming. They own land, they have cattle, and access to water and fresh air."

"Yes," I added, "the question we need to ask ourselves is how does one measure poverty? A child with holes in their shirt is not necessarily poor—their shirt could have gotten ripped as they were out playing. You have families who are land proprietors, who provide their own food and make their own clothing, but they might be seen walking barefoot or with dust on their clothing given the climate in which they live. Does that mean we should take pictures of them and label them as poverty-stricken?"

By the end of lunch, we were all convinced that the "Walk for Water" posters were lacking in context and served to perpetuate a one-sided narrative of Africa. {I do not, by any means, intend to diminish the efforts of the organizers. Indeed, there are people in Africa, as elsewhere, who do not have access to safe drinking water. #IndigenousCanadianReserves. I am simply advocating for a critical analysis of the way such charitable efforts for Africa are presented.}

Again, my point: Blackness is "messiah-fied" at best (the Black History Month posters) and "stigmatized" and "nullified" at worst (A Walk for Water),[9] but never just "normalized" like the whitewashed walls of my high school.

#HighSchoolAndTheBlackBody

---

9   Now that I am a bit older, I feel bad for having been so critical of their efforts given that they were young students trying to make a difference in this world that is so in need of change. However, in the context I was in at the time, the Black Body was constantly being degraded or objectified. Therefore, all of it—whether *Kony 2012* assemblies or charitable initiatives for Africa—became irritating and I found myself ready to snap at people. I do believe it is important to educate privileged people about global issues, though in a fashion that is sensitive to the victims in question.

ON SCHOOL SPIRIT DAYS
28 MARCH 2014

It is frightening how lightness can so easily whirl into an
unbearable heaviness, and how heaviness can cause so
much pain. —AWAD IBRAHIM, "One Is Not Born Black"

Today is "Western Day." On my way to the guidance
office this morning . . . you know, I'm not even sure
why it's called "guidance." I feel they "guide-down" the
students . . . anyway, on my way there, I crossed paths
with one of the student government leaders all dressed up
Western style and looking giddy. She asked a staff member
walking down the hall, "Where's your Western?" The lady
was clearly unaware of the spirit day, as I always am.

"They didn't say anything about it on the phone calls?" the
student asked.

It was Friday, March 21, the the United Nations International Day for the Elimination of Racism, but of course, at
my school it was "Happy Day!" In Commemoration of Happy
Day, student government posted inspirational quotes on the
lockers of all the students:

"You're awesome!"

"Those shoes were a really good call!"

"You're beautiful."

"Smile."

Actually, I frowned. Nope, Happy Day didn't sway me!

Student government puts a lot of effort into organizing these spirit days, brainstorming a theme, drawing posters, and making announcements. The purpose of a school spirit day is to build the *spirit* of the student body, to unite them through a particular theme, for example, happiness or Western wear. How can the Black student possibly be happy on the "Happy" spirit day when her school ignores an international day for the elimination of something as real as racism? Something she experiences daily inside and outside of the classroom? Happy Day was a mockery *deh*!

For commemorations such as this one (the International Day for the Elimination of Racism) I could have—as with the absence of Black History Month at my school—taken it upon myself to approach senior administration and query the school's lack of involvement in such crucial events. But does the school have to be reminded to host a Remembrance Day assembly (which most students believe are mandatory)? I skip them (will write about that at a later time). The answer is no. Well, anti-racism or Black History Month events are just as important. So why must I constantly remind? Recognizing Black History Month is legislated by the provincial government. This is why I'm annoyed with the school. Senior administration is neglecting its duty to the students.

#MyStruggle

#ELEVATORUSEAGAIN
1 APRIL 2014

We realize the importance of our voices
only when we are silenced.

—MALALA YOUSAFZAI, *I Am Malala*

just left history class. On my way up to my English literature class on the second floor, I pressed the button for the elevator when a young teacher in a bright pink sweater stormed my way:

"Excuse me, you can't use the elevator!" she says, raging.

"No. I have a pass," I say. She doesn't even listen.

"No! I don't care. C'mon!" she says, snapping her fingers at me. "Take the stairs!" Finally, she got a hold over her barking self and said, "Do you have a card?"

Had she listened to me a sentence ago, she wouldn't have made herself look like such an utter imbecile.

"Yes, I do," I said coolly.

"Let's see," she said roughly.

I presented my pass.

"Who gave it to you?" she said, peering at my pass suspiciously.

I should have told her that I smuggled it from the office. She turned around and briskly walked away when she saw that my vice principal had signed off on my elevator pass. *What a bitch*, I thought. I got on the elevator and chuckled to myself. She clearly is not happy with herself. The woman snapped at me and pointed in the direction of the stairwell. "C'mon!" she said, as if I were a dog. I am mad. I will be going to my vice principal right after this class to express my discontent. I guess it is unfortunate that something as trivial as an elevator pass can drive someone into a roughly two-minute conniption. I consider it to be a vital indication of the skewed nature of our priorities as a society. *Sigh*.

#ShakingHead[10]

---

10   My moments in the elevator with overly inquisitive teachers were obviously very frustrating. To me, each elevator incident was a racial micro-aggression. Of course, one can argue that there was gender or age discrimination at play. However, in this world, Black people have been trained to be Black first. Therefore, when I was the target of any unreasonable discrimination, I experienced it as a Black student first. Ultimately, each elevator incident made me a stronger person, more aware of myself, my rights and position, and society. Nonetheless, I could have done without the constant surveillance and policing that came with my use of the elevator. It was demoralizing. My right to be in that space was always questioned. As Blacks, we're already so policed in the wider world—when shopping, when going through airport security, when walking or when driving. School is the last place where I would want to experience more policing. I understand that teachers have the right to question what they deem questionable; however, like in the case of Ms. Pink Sweater, they were downright abusive.

JUST ANOTHER REFLECTION ABOUT SCHOOL

5 APRIL 2014

You may encounter many defeats
but you must not be defeated.

—MAYA ANGELOU

I never got to ask my guidance counsellor about her one nominee per school concern. She was speaking with someone when I went to retrieve my form after school that day (March 28). I also never got to complain to my vice principal about Ms. Pink Sweater teacher because she was out that day (April 1). However, I will follow up in due time. I don't know what is driving my guidance counsellor to respond to me in that way. It makes me feel as if I do not deserve to be that one nominee from my school, and why don't I? These micro-aggressions are the worst and they must not go unacknowledged. The irony is that they're often committed by staff—teachers, counsellors, administrators—those who are (by job description) employed to be in learning spaces called schools to teach, guide, and attend to the needs and concerns of students.

I consider it very unfortunate when a student is aware of the sheer pretension of the staff and the institutions they serve. I still cannot believe that teacher barked at me like that about the elevator. She treated me inhumanely, disrespectfully. I wonder how she would have reacted if I were someone else. Someone else—perhaps one of her fellow staff members, a student in a wheelchair, a visible adult, a white person. I'm sure she would not have reacted in the way that she did to me.

At my school, there are visibly and non-visibly disabled students who use the elevator. Their use of it is never questioned. My use of it is continually questioned by some of my own teachers and by other members of staff. Their inquiries are not as simple as "Can I see your elevator pass?" or "Do you have an elevator pass?" Their inquiries are invasive, often resulting in me being told that I am not responding to their invasion of my privacy in a "respectful" way. As if they were engaging me in a respectful way. Who do some of these teachers think they are? Why do they exploit their power, and feel entitled to degrade and stigmatize students? They themselves need to be taught.

THE GRAD HOUSE INCIDENT
7 APRIL 2014

Human rights are not things that are put on the table for people to enjoy. These are things you fight for and then you protect.

—WANGARI MAATHAI

On Thursday, April 3, 2014, I was invited to attend the Annual General Meeting (AGM) of Dalhousie's African Student Association (DASA). DASA had planned to hold a film screening and spoken word presentations following the AGM. The event was held at the Grad House—a social club on campus. The house consists of a café and a games room on the ground floor and meeting rooms on the top floor. I arrived early to help with set-up for the event. I met the head of DASA there upon arriving. She was busy trying to locate the manager of the Grad House who had said he'd be there early to help her with some logistics. He was MIA and DASA's president was pissed.

"I don't get this. We reserved the place for our event. I spoke with him prior about being here early to help with set-up, and he's not here . . . uggh," she says, sighing in frustration.

My friend, Sana, and I thought to grab some warm beverages from the café. The barista told me she couldn't "do hot chocolate." Hmm, I thought—a little bizarre—but I didn't really ponder her response. "You have to talk to her," she said, indicating the chef who was busy cooking in the back, "if you want hot chocolate."

I swiveled around to the counter separating customers from the kitchen. "Hi," I said to the chef, "can you make me hot chocolate? She said to come to you for hot chocolate."

"What?" said the puzzled chef, addressing the barista.

"Well, yeah. I see that you're busy back there and I don't want to get in your way."

"Well, you know," he said, "you'd have to take the money from her anyway if I'm to make the hot chocolate, so I don't see why you can't process her order."

A detailed discussion ensued; the barista indignantly pressing her case as to why she could not take my order for hot chocolate; the chef, rightfully annoyed, elucidating the ludicrousness of her claim.

"Habiba," Sana chimes in, "do you want to grab something from Tim Hortons?"

"Sure." And off to Tim Hortons we went. The Grad House was too embroiled in a dispute about job roles to "do me my hot chocolate."

"You know, Habiba, I can't help but think it's racism," Sana says.[11] "That's extremely bizarre. You go to purchase a drink and there's this big fuss about making it."

---

11   I know this might sound paranoid to some readers but read on.

"At first, I didn't really get what the barista meant by she 'couldn't do hot chocolate,'" I said. "I wondered if they had run out of hot chocolate? Was she physically incapable of making it? Clearly, neither possibility was true for her. And then to think that she would actually get into a huge discussion with the chef over why she didn't want to go back there and make me the hot chocolate. That was really disrespectful to me as a customer. Anyway, thank you for catching on and pulling me out of there. Our money is better spent elsewhere."

We headed back to the Grad House for the AGM. The latest from the manager was that he'd be there at seven although our event began at six in the evening.

Before the meeting started, Sana asked me to do a photo for her "How Would You React?" Campaign. The campaign intends to spread awareness about the micro- and macro-aggressions of racism experienced by students of colour at Dalhousie University.

I gladly accepted, and we went by one of the meeting rooms at the back where I quickly reflected and came up with this message to include with my picture:

"How would you react if you were told that people like 'yourself' should be grateful to go to school?"

The AGM went well and proved to be a good learning experience for me, giving me insights on university society politics. The president gave a review of what the society did this year. Society members expressed and debated their thoughts and concerns about the famous Africa Night that takes place every year, and new executive members were elected. Afterwards, I stayed upstairs with my friend and a few other people who were taking pictures for the "How Would You React?" campaign, while the others went down to the café for the spoken word part of the night.

I made a few rounds up and down the stairs, and on one instance, as I went through the door separating the top level from the bottom, I met aggressive resistance from a group of graduate students who were drinking beer and playing pool in the room adjacent to the door. They did not want me to walk through the room into the café. They wanted me, and all the others who were there with DASA, to exit through the back entrance and walk outside along the winding stretch of the patio and enter through the main door. The former route was two seconds, while the latter longer, cold (yes Halifax in April is *cold*), and unnecessary. I refused, informing them that I was merely walking through the room into the café. They did not own the space; DASA had the Grad House reserved for the occasion. In response to my retaliation, one guy said, "It's okay, they [meaning the Grad House employees] are gonna come lock the door soon." Lock the door they did indeed.

Those who were still upstairs were made to walk around in the cold in order to enter the café. They were locked out; relegated to the back entrance; DASA members who had reserved the space for their *own* AGM. We were met by security at the front entrance. Since when does the Grad House have security for its events? Right as I got past, Wambui, DASA's president, stormed down the hall, her body shaking, tears streaming down her face, her hand waving in protest. "I can't take this!" she screams.

"Wambui, what's going on?" I ask.

"They're trying to deny me my culture! I won't let them!" she says, distressed. "Don't talk to me! No one talk to me!" she shouts at a crowd of people who've gathered behind her.

Three white students had complained to the barista—Ms. I Can't Do Hot Chocolate—about the poetry of the invited guest for the night, Leila Jones. Her poetry addresses critical themes pertaining to the appropriation of Black culture and identity by white people. The complainants cried "reverse racism," saying that they did not feel "comfortable" with her lyrics. Ms. I Can't Do Hot Chocolate approached Wambui and demanded that Leila be removed from the stage, and that Wambui apologize to the three students who felt offended. Wambui rightfully refused. She told Ms. I Can't Do Hot Chocolate that in her culture it is disrespectful to interrupt an elder when she is speaking. By "elder" she was acknowledging Leila's slight seniority in age. She went on to say that the students who were offended could leave if they felt it necessary.

I quickly went to Leila who was sitting calmly in the café taking in the other performances.

"Leila, I think you should go check out what's happening. Wambui's freaking out," I told her, aware that she was probably the most mature (age-wise) person in attendance for the DASA event; hoping that she would know how to manage the situation.

"Okay," Leila said as she got up to go investigate. I stayed and listened to Fiker who was now up on stage reciting a love poem. Too disturbed by the image of Wambui screaming and distressed, I eventually went back up to see how things were unfolding.

DASA had the space reserved for the evening—in other words, had the space reserved *for* Leila's poetry on cultural appropriation and for any content DASA wanted to include—and had over forty persons in attendance versus the three complainants. #Let'sGetReal. The barista said to Wambui, "You know you could lose your funding for this," insinuating that she would report the "offence" to Dalhousie, resulting in DASA losing all monetary support from the institution.

We were subsequently approached by security who told us to "tone it down"—Black cultural appropriation is too much of a *heavy* topic to be discussed. The barista complained to them. Instead of attempting to settle it with Wambui in a respectful way, she deemed it necessary to have security wield their authority. #PolicingTheBlackBody

"Oh no," I said, "this is bad, really bad. DASA had the space reserved for the event, and this is the treatment we get? You really should do something about this, Wambui, don't leave it at this. The barista needs to be held accountable because this is unacceptable. It's as if as Blacks we can't even live; we can't even speak about our own experiences in spaces that we pay for."

"What should I do?" she asked.

"You need to write down everything. The day, the time, where this happened [at the Grad House], what it was that happened," I responded.

Leila and a member from the Dalhousie Student Union (DSU) agreed to go upstairs to help Wambui strategize. We were not about to bow to racism and intimidation. Once they came back downstairs and things had seemingly settled, I asked Leila if she was ready to go. She was going to drop me home. She told me that she wanted to stay for a bit to see how the event progressed in case the barista and the other graduate students became vicious and bully-like once she left. The DASA attendees were all undergraduate students, some of whom actually apologized to the barista and the other students out of fear. They did not want to get "in trouble" later on. Soon, we left, the Grad House filled with tension, the event gone sour.

The next day I sent a message to Wambui:

> Sorry everything had to transpire like that. (But, as Leila was telling me, it's for the better . . . there's positive to everything.)
>
> I like how you didn't give in, settle, apologize etc. You did the right thing, and I get your frustration.

She responded saying:

> Hey Habiba thank you so much for coming and that's true. We've started a movement and this issue must be addressed. Thank you. It took much restraint not to get even more upset about what was happening! Have you seen Leila's letter? It's fantastic.

The Grad House incident was merely an expression of an underlying, deeper dystopic reality of racism that is known to many Black students on campuses and high schools across the world.

#SystemicRacismAndTheBlackBody

During the course of the weeks that followed, Wambui, Leila, Sana, and I met to discuss and formulate a petition, write letters to the university's administration, and speak with local media about the events that transpired that night. Community activists, professors, and other students joined us in our call to address the systemic, institutionalized racism on campus. The petition looked like this:

> We suggest the following steps be taken by the University in order to demonstrate that they take these events seriously and are committed to working with Black students to ensure our equity on campus:
>
> 1. Disciplinary action is taken against the Grad House employee.
>
> 2. An official apology from the Grad House and from the employee.
>
> 3. A commitment to meet with students across campus in order to discuss strategies and measures for preventing these types of incidents.
>
> 4. Active engagement from Dalhousie University and the Dalhousie Student Union in the planning and execution of DASA's initiatives.

5. We believe that cultural visibility, education, and accessibility are needed on campus. To ensure this we believe that funding should be provided to the DASA, to the Black Student Advising Centre (BSAC), to the James R. Robinson Johnston Chair in Black Studies, and to the Black Faculty Collective to enable us to host educational events regarding issues faced by Black students, cultural events that promote understanding, and artistic events that foster relationships.

6. A commitment from the university with a strong timeline to create a Black Studies Major within the next two years.

7. A commitment from the Dalhousie University Administration and the Office of the President to meet quarterly with the James R. Robinson Johnston Chair in Black Studies, the Black Faculty Collective, and student representatives to create collaborative solutions to address the issues of Black students on campus.

8. To recognize these matters before the end of the school year: April 26, 2014.

Some of the requests in the petition are still a work in progress. However, Ms. I Can't Do Hot Chocolate (the Grad House employee) has been fired. Apparently, we were not the first group of clients she had harassed. The appropriate offices and departments at the university have been meeting with Black students and faculty to discuss anti-racism strategies. And as of the 2014 fall semester, all Dalhousie students will have to participate in mandatory anti-racism training sessions as part of orientation week.

What we experienced that night was devastating, but sometimes adversity is a necessary precursor to meaningful change. In this case, change is the acknowledgement of the experiences of Black students on campus and a commitment to eliminating the racism they experience.

#VictoryAtLast

APPRECIATE THE UNFORTUNATE
15 APRIL 2014

Sometimes people try to destroy you, precisely because
they recognize your power—not because they don't see it,
but because they see it and they don't want it to exist.

—BELL HOOKS

nother day at school. It's funny, I was on my way up to English class (#ElevatorAgain) when I saw one of the teachers who challenged my use of the elevator walking near it. I slowed down as I approached the elevator. *Oh God spare me*, I thought to myself. I did not want another barking session. I was slightly relieved when I saw her turn the corner. I got on the elevator and away to English class I went.

By the way, I did speak to my vice principal about the constant harassment from teachers about my use of the elevator. I did not find our conversation wholly satisfying. To her credit, she did send out a mass email to all the staff asserting that elevator passes are not "given out like candy," and that students who use the elevator are aware of the privilege that they've been given . . . *Oh Lord, when elevator use becomes a "privilege" what has the world come to?* Anyway, she concluded the meeting by saying that she thinks that will quell some of the teachers' suspicion of my *illicit*—as they see it—elevator use. I sure hope it does.

Here's what I did not find wholly satisfying about how she addressed my concern: When I told her of Ms. Pink Sweater's (the teacher who barked and snapped at me) degrading and uncivilized treatment of my attempt to use the elevator, she told me that I must "appreciate the unfortunate." The "unfortunate" meaning that Ms. Pink Sweater had probably just come off duty and that she was probably a little frustrated given that there are students who goof around and try to use the elevator when they're really not entitled to. I said Ms. Pink Sweater's treatment of the situation (well there really was no "situation." Ms. Pink Sweater problematized my mundane elevator use and created a "situation") reinforced my awareness of the teacher-student hierarchies that exist in this school—perhaps in all schools. Regardless of where the hierarchies exist, my point is that the one existing here (at W.H. High School) is toxic. My vice principal was considerate, however matter-of-fact. She persisted with the "appreciate the unfortunate" discourse, ultimately ending our conversation, ultimately absolving Ms. Pink Sweater of her responsibility to act in a courteous and sensible fashion, and ultimately solidifying my not-so-pleasant thoughts of high school and the Black Body.

I think she should have dealt with my concern by allowing me to identify Ms. Pink Sweater, and she could therefore have approached her, perhaps asked her to apologize to me (I know the apology piece is a little idealistic—since when do teachers apologize to students?), but she should have essentially brought my discontent with Ms. Pink Sweater's barking at me to Ms. Pink Sweater's attention.

How do administrators expect students to have a sense of belonging at what is supposedly our school if teachers, guidance counsellors, and other members of staff get away with inhumane treatment of students? Maybe they don't expect us to have a sense of belonging and perhaps that is why the racism in school goes unchecked. #FoodForThought

BLACK STUDENTS: AN ECONOMY OVERLOOKED

15 APRIL 2014

We must dare to invent the future.

—THOMAS SANKARA

Every year, Canadians pay billions of dollars in taxes to the national budget for education. Parents, teachers, and students are all actors in this "educational economy." These individuals have income-earning potential and contribute to the economy by spending daily on products ranging from textbooks to hairpins.

Blacks are nonetheless in an extremely ironic economic position: Black Canadian taxpayers are important actors in the national economy; yet, Black students are subjected to overwhelmingly whitewashed and racist school curricula and bureaucracies despite their large contributions to the education industry. Black Canadian taxpayers are paying to feed their children an intensely racist and epistemically violent education.

Where do other non-Black, particularly white, Canadian taxpayers stand in this dynamic? Their economic position is no different from that of Black taxpayers in the sense that they too pay to harm the psyches of fellow citizens. It is not sufficient for white parents and taxpayers to be concerned only about the educational experiences of their own children. They cannot continue to overlook the white and Eurocentric curriculum—one that is steeped in white privilege and hegemony—which dominates the pedagogy in Canadian schools.

School is purported to be a place of intellectual and personal growth. Many teachers will tell you that they feel they naturally fulfill this responsibility of "shaping students' intellects and encouraging their personal growth." I argue that this responsibility is not met when it comes to the teaching of Black students. As I have said several times before, the curriculum is whitewashed; hence, school will encourage the intellectual growth of Black students, but it will be from a biased perspective.

The school "culture"—as discussed in a previous chapter—is not conducive to the personal growth of Black students. If teachers and administrators were to truly assume this responsibility for *all* students, they would critically analyze their ideologies about Blackness and the way they deliver every subject, from maths to history. Teachers would begin to ask themselves questions such as the following:

- What does it mean to have Black students share classroom space with white students in light of racist legacies—like the murders of Renisha

McBride and Trayvon Martin—which still persist today?

- What does it mean to teach Black students who carry heavy burdens linked to their culture, identity, and loss thereof? Students who are continually omitted and erased in textbooks and curricula, students who seldom see themselves represented in visually and politically important spaces in society, spaces like television commercials, films, billboards, and even the parliament?

- What kind of responsibility do I have for Black students in a world where powerful media images stigmatizing Black youth are so pervasive?

- What kind of responsibility do I have for Black students who, as a group, are more likely to drop out of high school than any other race?

I do wonder who cares about Black students. Why are our educational needs and human rights—*our right to dignity, our right to be innocent until proven guilty*—placed significantly below those of white students' rights?

Where is the accountability? Who is accountable to Black students? Who is accountable to my brother, my sister, and myself for the thirteen (combined) years we spent in high school? It has been thirteen years of having our bodies hurt, stigmatized, hindered, and nullified in "democratic" institutions of learning. As a Black high school student, I am a stakeholder in my education and in my school, and so are my teachers, so is my principal, my vice principal, my guidance counsellor, and my program coordinator. Do they not have a responsibility towards me? A responsibility towards my human rights, my dignity, and my security of person? A responsibility to ensure that I walk into school every morning feeling that I belong, trusting that I will receive a curriculum that will suit my educational needs and contribute to my self-actualization? Why are my basic human rights eroded by the very institution that is meant to build my confidence, educate me, and provide me with a quality education?

"TU VIENS D'OÙ?"
30 APRIL 2014

A studied silence on race acts as a wall,
blocking people in Canada from each other.
—VICKY MOCHAMA, broadcaster[12]

I was sitting in my first-period history class this morning, or *Histoire* because I take the class in French. My teacher was chatting amicably with her colleague. I was the only student present. The others had yet to arrive. We are about to commence exams; hence, very few students come to class these days. Her colleague and I eventually began chatting about the weather—*snow at the end of April?!*

---

12 I love the quote I used to open this chapter. We need to have conversations about race and whiteness in Canada to fully embrace and understand each other as Canadians. I love my country and am disheartened each time someone (usually white) tries to place me outside of it. Such displacement sours—for the Black person—any interaction that was initially light-hearted and friendly. Why is it that white Canadians, many of whose grandparents arrived on ships from Europe during the Second World War, take for granted that they are true Canadians while they make us not *feel* Canadian?

Before leaving she casually asked me, *"Tu viens d'où?"* Where are you from?

"Who, me?"

"Oui."

My teacher chimed in, "Oh no. She's from here," meaning Canada, "she was just in Ontario before."

She just presumed that I have not *been* here. It reminded me of the time the doctor at the walk-in clinic asked me the same question, and then said, "Oh, sorry. I presumed you were an immigrant." At least he was honest.

Perhaps they were hoping for something more exotic like Kenya or Chad. Liberia maybe? Not even Jamaica, Habiba? C'mon, I could have at least claimed my parents' nationalities to give them some satisfaction.

#TheOther

EPISTEMIC VIOLENCE
THROUGH SELECTED TEXTS
FOR ENGLISH COURSES

6 MAY 2014

> White people use their literature to maintain culture.
> That's why you find references to Milton and Spencer
> and Shakespeare and Dostoyevsky in contemporary novels.
>
> —NTOZAKE SHANGE

xample: *The Great Gatsby*

TOM: "Civilization's going to pieces . . . Have you read "The Rise of the Coloured Empires" . . . ?"

#ScientificRacism

TOM: "The idea is if we don't look out the white race will be--will be utterly submerged. It's all scientific stuff; it's been proved. . . . It's up to us who are the dominant race to watch out or these other races will have control of things."

DAISY: "We've got to beat them down."

TOM: "... we're Nordics.... and we've produced all the things that go to make civilization—oh, science and art and all that."[13]

This is Higher-Level English class reading material. Yes, there is something inherently wrong with studying such material for a final exam when it is delivered and read without any context. Furthermore, for the Black student, there is something inherently grotesque with her classmates studying such material without any context. Imagine: a group of roughly twenty-five students crouched over their desks silently ingesting the book's content to prepare for end-of-month exams.

#HighSchoolAndTheBlackBody

---

13   F. Scott Fitzgerald, *The Great Gatsby* (Atlântico Press, 2013), 9.

OBSTETRIC FISTULA: A BLACK WOMAN'S BURDEN?[14]

24 MAY 2014

I have borne thirteen children, and seen most all
sold off to slavery, and when I cried out with my mother's grief,
none but Jesus heard me! And ain't I a woman?

—SOJOURNER TRUTH

Yesterday was the second annual International Day to End Obstetric Fistula. May 23, 2013, marked the first international day. Fistula is a devastating childbirth injury that occurs when a woman is in labour for a prolonged period and the baby is unable to come out. The baby eventually comes out but causes a hole to form between her bladder and vagina, or her bladder and rectum (in severe cases

---

14   I totally understand that obstetric fistula, a medical condition, is not unique to Black women. However, the majority of current fistula cases occur in Sub-Saharan Africa. I must add that when I first began advocating for this condition, it spoke so strongly to me as a young Black woman. Therefore, again, I know that this is not a "Black" condition but one that disproportionately affects Black/ African women.

between both). This hole is known as an "obstetric fistula." Due to where the fistula is located in the affected woman, she will constantly leak urine, feces, or both.

Today, I organized an event to commemorate the International Day to End Obstetric Fistula through my organization—the Women's Health Organization International (WHOI). The evening featured presentations and performances from community members, women's health activists, and participants from a program I started last month called the Fistula and Empowerment Program (FEP). Speakers touched on themes such as the causes of obstetric fistula and the importance of providing maternal health care facilities during a difficult labour. There were also poetry and dance performances.

One of the goals of the program is to underscore that there is no mutual exclusiveness between obstetric fistula experienced by African women and the health disparities faced by the program participants themselves, but rather that the experiences of both demographic groups are indicative of a bigger problem: the global condition of women and the health inequalities experienced by Black women in particular. During our program sessions, I often discuss the obscure history of obstetric fistula in North America, a history that comes as a shock to many simply because it is hard to fathom that an illness so devastating existed in this part of the world up until the mid-twentieth century.

One of the stories I focus on during my presentation is that of Anarcha, an African American slave who worked on the Wescott Plantation in Alabama in the mid-nineteenth century, around 1845. After several days of prolonged labour, Anarcha developed an obstetric fistula. She could not control her discharge of urine and feces. She smelled; she was unable to perform her duties on the plantation, and, given that her fistula compromised her worth as a slave, her master sold her to a gynecologist, Dr. Marion Sims.

At the time, Dr. Sims was innovating ways to cure fistula. Anarcha was one of a few other slave women who were sold like chattel to Sims to have their bodies experimented on like guinea pigs as he attempted to find a cure. Sims forcibly performed over thirty fistula surgeries on Anarcha without the use of anaesthesia (which was available at the time). Finally, her fistula was cured.

Even now, there is a shortage of fistula awareness in North America. What's interesting, however, is that it is an affliction that has a chilling yet revolutionary history in North American obstetric care. These vicious procedures revolutionized North American obstetric care by effectively giving rise to the technique now used to treat fistula.[15] Sims built a legacy for himself as a renowned gynecologist and fistula surgeon at the expense of Black women's lives. In 1855, he established a fistula hospital in New York, which later became known as The Women's Hospital. Sims is often quoted in medical textbooks as being the "father of gynecology" and his statue looms over the perimeters of Central Park, New York City.

---

15   Sara Spettel and Mark Donald White, "The Portrayal of J. Marion Sims' Controversial Surgical Legacy," *Journal of Urology* 185, no. 6 (June 2011): 2424–7. doi: 10.1016/j.juro.2011.01.077.

One of the paradoxes of obstetric fistula today is that a large number of fistula patients are Black women in Africa. So, even though the technique used to treat fistula was developed at the expense of Black slave women like Anarcha, their modern-day sisters have not benefitted from that sacrifice. #FistulaAndTheBlackBody

Sims is lauded in various modern and historical media, his legacy a questionable one. I salute the spirit of Anarcha instead. #MotherOfGynecology

#FistulaChampion

ON REMEMBRANCE DAY ASSEMBLIES

24 MAY 2014

Black history is not just for Black people—
Black history is Canadian history.

—JEAN AUGUSTINE

I was just reading a chapter in *When Jail Beats School: One Year in the Life of a Teacher* by Bairu Sium. It is an autobiographical novel about his experience teaching in the Toronto District School Board (TDSB) and many of the day-to-day struggles faced by his students. In the chapter "No One Wins War," he writes:

> A Canadian history textbook I once used had some unsavoury comments about Black West African conscripts who were forced to fight for France on the Western Front during WWI: During the attack, French-African troops positioned beside the Canadians broke ranks and fled from the poisonous gas at Vimy Ridge.

The Germans then came pouring through the hole in the line. The Canadians, with makeshift gas masks, managed to hold their position and eventually closed the gap in the line.[16]

#CurricularEurocentricism

Sium continues, analyzing discrepancies between the white and Black soldiers:

Did they really run? If they did, who could blame them? Perhaps they would have been better heroes if they had fought their way out of France and back to their own countries of Niger, Mali, and Senegal. Paradoxically, the same statement shows the injustices imperialism imposed on its pawns . . . The French, Canadians, and British were there because they had enlisted freely, until about 1916. The West Africans were there under duress.[17]

The excerpt reminded me of my own relationship to Remembrance Day and the mainstream, institutional, commemorative representations of the First and Second World Wars. I stopped attending Remembrance Day Assemblies last year in the eleventh grade. Had I been more aware at the time, I would have stopped going to the assemblies several years ago.

---

16   Bairu Sium, *When Jail Beats School: One Year in the Life of a Teacher* (Toronto: On the Edge Press Inc., 2012), 21.

17   Sium, 83.

In the second grade, my Aftercare[18] supervisor insisted that my granduncle could not have fought in the Second World War. He was an African, a Guinean, and the World Wars—*as we already know*—did not involve the lives of Africans. #SoNotTrue. I remember my eight-year-old self feeling indignant. I felt offended that in such a nonchalant and authoritative manner she could deny my granduncle's participation in the war. Again, I was eight years old. It was the second grade. It was November, the month of poppies, of sitting in large circles in the classroom as our teacher read, "In Flanders fields the poppies blow / Between the crosses, row on row. . ." of filing into the school gym for momentous assemblies about the strife the brave allies encountered on the frontlines. It was an exciting time. An important time. A time when fellow students shared stories about the horrors their grandfathers experienced in the war. Naturally, I wanted to make my claim to the war. Hence my recounting of the story of my granduncle, only to have my confidence deflated. I remember the relief I felt when my father finally arrived to take me home.

#TheNullificationOfBlackExperiences

---

18 A place where students would go in elementary school to wait for their parents to pick them up, a sort of daycare except happening at the end of the school day.

#MYEMAILTOTHEMINISTER

27 MAY 2014

> I raise up my voice—not so I can shout but so that
> those without a voice can be heard . . . . We cannot
> succeed when half of us are held back.
>
> —MALALA YOUSAFZAI

Hello there,

I am a high school student—who will be graduating this year—and would like to share my insights regarding what can be improved in the system.

I am pleased to know that the minister is reviewing the education system at present. I have attended Nova Scotia public high school for two years, and honestly, I have had a very frustrating experience mainly due to poor race relations/the lack thereof, and a complete absence of cultural competency on the part of staff/administrators and many students.

I am an International Baccalaureate (IB) student and I am very familiar with the program's commitment to developing concerned global citizens with strong intercultural awareness. As per their mission, they want ". . . to develop inquiring, knowledgeable and caring young people who help to create a better and more peaceful world through intercultural understanding and respect."

In my high school experience, the intercultural understanding and "respect" piece has expressed itself in stigmatizing the experiences and inaccurately portraying the realities of people in the non-Western world (this being done by IB students themselves, and endorsed by IB teachers). I understand that the IB program is an entity separate from the Department of Education. Nonetheless, it is a program offered at schools under the supervision of the Department of Education (schools which boast of the work, talent, and intercultural awareness of their IB students). Hence the urgent need for the department to take these points into account.

Something I found quite disturbing about my IB experience at W.H. High School was that I am one of three Black students in my Grade 12 cohort of about seventy in spite of the fact that W.H. has a significant Black student population and boasts of being "the most multicultural school east of Montreal." In the current Grade 11 cohort, there is only one Black student.

On that note, I think it is critical that the Board of Education, as well as staff and administrators at W.H., ask themselves what they mean by "most multicultural school east of Montreal." Multicultural in what sense: student population? That is indeed true. However, the staff and administrative bodies do not reflect this multiculturalism, which is frequently boasted about by the school. I find the school to be lacking the necessary tools to engage the "multiculturalism" it so loves to claim. Every day, W.H. sees new students arriving from Nepal, Congo, Rwanda, Cuba etc. Still, the staff remains white. Still, they offend, ridicule, and degrade students of colour and immigrant students.

I have had several of my own personal encounters with racism and degradation by teachers at the school (I have decided to spare you them for this letter). The teachers are largely ignorant of the Black experience—or any other non-white experience for that matter—and do not seem interested in re-evaluating their knowledge. Yet, their classes are made up of students (like myself) who do not relate to Eurocentric experiences but who are made to learn, theorize, write about, and study experiences foreign to our own realities. Meanwhile, our experiences, our realities are sidelined. The educational system is indeed not truly representative of all its students.

A lot of these issues stem from the Eurocentric approach to learning. There used to be an African Canadian Studies course at W.H. (this was before I arrived there) but it was cut due to "funding issues." Still, courses like Mi'kmaq and African Canadian Studies that are offered by some schools (W.H. does have a Mi'kmaq program) are not part of the core curriculum. By that I mean that they are usually (if not always) offered as electives. This would not be problematic if the important themes taught in such classes made their way into history or English classes that are part of the core curriculum. However, they do not (and if they do, it's usually as part of some optional unit assignment).

I have many thoughts on the issue and how the minister could create real, systemic, curricular change for a more holistic, racially inclusive, educational system. The reflections above are merely a synopsis—a telling one nonetheless, and a call for fast, critical, and effective change.

A few key strategies that quickly come to mind:

1. Anti-racist training for staff and administrators.

2. Development of critical tools and strategies to engage students of non-white backgrounds.

3. Review of the core curriculum by experts in epistemological racism.

Best regards,
Habiba Cooper Diallo

PART III

ON WEARING
THE KENTE SASH

2 JUNE 2014

Not everything that is faced can be changed,
but nothing can be changed until it is faced.

—JAMES BALDWIN

"But why should I wear the Kente sash?" I asked my mom, "For the whole school year there is no recognition of 'African-ness,' and then suddenly at graduation when African/Black students are leaving, we are encouraged to wear the Kente sash?"

Tomorrow, I will be having my graduation for successfully completing the IB Diploma program. Later in June, there will be another graduation at which I will receive my provincial high school diploma. Starting around January/February, the daily morning announcements included an "If you are African Nova Scotian and would like to wear the Kente sash at graduation please come to the main office and let one of the secretaries know."

I chuckled every time I heard that announcement. It just sounded so awkward. Firstly, what on earth is a "Kente sash" for those who do not know? And what does being African Nova Scotian have to do with wearing the Kente sash? I guess my frustration with the invitation to wear the sash is that while it does symbolize African culture, in the context of the nullification of African and Black culture in school, it appears to be a surface level remembrance.

The Department of Education has an academic scholarship for African Canadian students. A few months ago—during one of my regular scavenger hunts in the guidance office—I found one of the applications sitting in a dusty pile at the bottom of a bookcase. I quickly informed my other African Canadian / Black peers, distributing copies to a few of them. You will automatically get the scholarship if you have an over 75 percent average. #AWinIndeed. So, what's more important: advertising the sash for months leading up to graduation, or advertising the scholarship?

MY IB GRADUATION
AND THE BLACK BURDEN

3 JUNE 2014

Goodbyes are only for those who love with their eyes.
Because for those who love with heart and soul
there is no such thing as separation.

—JALAL AD-DIN RUMI

Tonight was my IB graduation. All of the graduates along with their families and friends arrived at our school theatre at 7:00 p.m. for the ceremony. It was a heartfelt event overall. We slowly filed into the theatre and occupied the bulky red folding chairs. My principal gave his regards to the graduates, followed by the IB coordinator and then the African Nova Scotian representative for the Halifax Regional School Board. My mother had suggested to the principal that the African Nova Scotian representative sit on the stage with the other members of staff and also give salutations to the graduates. In her speech, the IB coordinator introduced all of the IB teachers. They stood as the audience applauded them for their effort in educating the students over the past two years of the IB Diploma Program. The IB teachers were all white, my graduating IB cohort predominantly white and Asian, save for three Black students.

Two students were called to the stage to say a few words on behalf of the cohort. Next, two other students were called up to present awards to the teachers as tokens of appreciation. Then began the presentation of IB pins to all the graduates, followed by academic awards in each of the Higher Level and Standard Level subjects. I walked across the stage in my Kente sash. Yes, I did wear it, and I wore it proudly. Although, throughout the whole school year, there was an erasure, a dismissal of the identity of Black students (an issue that urgently needs addressing), the Kente is a symbol of my difference, of my Blackness, of my Africanness; a symbol of the very unique experiences that I have had, different from the rest of the students in my cohort given the mere fact that I am Black. A fellow student also wore the sash. The two of us were Kente sash bearers tonight. On our graduating night. I won the Higher Level French Award. It was rewarding—an award for hard work. My dear teacher was very happy for me. I could see the joy radiating from her face as she bestowed it upon me.

After the ceremony, we all made our way to the cafeteria for pictures and a small reception. I left the auditorium sobbing. On my way out, I stopped to greet my Loyal Advisors, my family friends who have been with me through thick and thin on this journey. Upon encountering them, I was suddenly consumed by thoughts and vivid memories of my father at my eighth grade graduation. *Indeed, if he were here tonight, he would have been so proud. How I miss him.* My eyes welled up with tears as I smiled to greet them all, and they launched into their photographic campaign. Leila enveloped me in her arms and I began to cry. "Why are you crying?" she asked. "It's my dad," I said. "I miss him so much."

Habiba and friend, Bhagi, at her IB Graduation, 2014. Photo courtesy of the author.

After myriad photos and hugs in the cafeteria, we finally made our departure. The Loyal Advisors, my mother, and I were headed to a cozy restaurant downtown for a graduation night celebration dinner.

"Habiba," my friend said, "the event was so whitewashed."

"I know."

"It's kind of scary."

I laughed. "How is it scary? Did it make you fearful?" I asked. She commented upon the paucity of racial diversity in the IB program at my school and how she found it to be very disturbing considering the racial diversity of the school's overall student population and also given the IB program's mandate "to develop inquiring, knowledgeable and caring young people who help to create a better and more peaceful world through intercultural understanding and respect."

How can the IB student truly gain intercultural understanding and respect if they fail to critically engage with the host of non-Eurocentric cultures within their own school? is all I can think.

Once at the restaurant, the five of us settled into a nook and placed our orders. I had fish and chips—Maritime style. (They were all right . . . just all right.) Everyone congratulated me on my success. We quickly began to discuss pressing issues that are currently being faced by Black populations in Canada—the high incarceration rate among young Canadian Black males; the failure of the legal system to adequately advocate on their behalf; the incessant racism experienced by Black students at school.

Somewhere during our impassioned debates on these critical topics my friend said, "Hah. Would you believe it? I overheard the people sitting at the table across from us saying that they do not like what we're talking about. They are not comfortable with what we're saying." #GradHouseNo2

"It's like we can't even live. This is our life, our everyday experiences," another friend said.

"They can leave if they're not comfortable. Everywhere we go and discuss our life experiences, people try to silence us," I said.

"Furthermore, why are they listening to our conversation?" my mother asked. "Why are they so nosy?"

"As far as I'm concerned, this is a celebration! Graduation party! No negativity wanted!" I added.

Eventually, they did get up and leave. The Black burden is too much for the average white ear to bear. My mother insisted that we end the night on a positive note: "As Black people, our conversations are sometimes too gothic."

#NegativeDiscourseCycle. "Tonight is Habiba's graduation, so let us welcome her New Beginning with good wishes." They each gave a small tribute to me for the hard work and perseverance I demonstrated over the past four years in high school.

My Final Thoughts: Neither the teaching staff, nor IB students, are a true reflection of the student population at the school. Over and over again, staff and administration at the school will tell you that our school is "the most multicultural school east of Montreal." This is our school's claim to fame. The claim is a little bogus as far as I'm concerned. The student population might be ethnically the most diverse at any school east of Montreal. However, the staff and administrative populations are surely not, nor is the "Academic Elite," in other words, the IB student population.

I am truly touched by the love and support I received from my mother and my dearest friends who came out to attend my graduation. That being said, there is a lot of work to be done in order to alleviate the Black burden at future IB graduations in Nova Scotia.

#HighSchoolAndTheBlackBurden

ON THE EDGE: A BLACK GIRL'S PURSUIT OF QUALITY HAIR CARE

16 JUNE 2014

I am not this hair. I am not this skin.

I am the soul that lives within.

—INDIA ARIE, "I AM NOT MY HAIR"

Tonight after work, I went to the salon to straighten my hair.

Yesterday, when I called the salon to make the appointment, my conversation with the stylist on the receiving end went something like this:

"So how much will it cost?" I asked.

"Well, it all depends on your hair. How curly is your hair?" he asked. Essentially—as per the guidelines at many salons nowadays—the price of a hair service is dependent upon the length of one's hair and the amount of time needed to do it.

"I have Black hair, so I'm actually wondering if any of your Black hair stylists will be in at that time."

"All of our stylists are trained to do diverse hair types," was the slightly indignant response I got from the other end. I couldn't help but chuckle to myself. *Oh really?* I thought. "Okay, well then see you tomorrow!"

My anxieties are warranted. Sometime last year, I had called the same salon to request the same service. Instead of asking outright for a Black hair stylist, I asked if they had any stylists available who knew how to work with "Afro" hair. I was subsequently disappointed when the stylist on the receiving end of the call said, "None of our stylists can do that kind of hair." My friend's mom was positively mad when I shared the story with her.

"You should have told them that you're offended by that comment! In that case, they should not be advertising as a hair salon. On the banner outside of the salon they should state specifically the types of hair they're capable of doing— Caucasian hair, Asian hair . . . if that's the case." She was right.

It is difficult, as Black women, to find a salon that will offer you quality service (good customer service, gentilesse, etc.) and that actually knows how to do your hair at the same time. You can find the two individually, as in a salon that offers quality service but whose hair stylists will jack-up your hair, or a salon whose stylists will give you a proper hairdo at the price of chronic neck pain.

When I got to the salon tonight, I was initially offended by the stylist's remarks: "I'll let you do this because I don't wanna hurt you." By "this" he was referring to loosening out—or "undoing" as some people say—my braids. The funny thing is, it was his ignorance about how to manage my hair that hurt me. Any Black person with natural hair can tell you that loosening braids does *not* hurt. It's as simple as using your fingers or a tool such as a pen to poke through and unwind the interlaced strands, essentially how you'd unwind interlaced strands of any hair texture.

Soon, he began to brush and part the sections of my hair. *Oh God*, I muttered under my breath, cringing when I saw what he was going to use to brush my hair. The brushing was ineffective, as I knew it would be, so I whipped out my trusted wide-toothed comb.[19] "Here, why don't you use this?" I suggested, handing him the comb. He said something about not wanting to hurt me again. I laughed to myself. "No, it doesn't hurt," I confirmed. "If you hold the section of the hair above the piece you're combing, I don't feel anything." *I hope he does the straightening right.*

To his credit, he did an excellent job and as it turned out, we came to genuinely appreciate each other's humanity by virtue of a deeply poignant conversation we had about social exclusion pertaining to his sexual orientation. He taught me

---

19   The brushing was ineffective due to the type of brush he was using, which would've only resulted in tugging my hair. I am happy that this stylist listened to me when I advised him. Many don't—their arrogance causes them to take offence. Sometimes if those offering a service or teaching a lesson were to chill out about being "criticized," everyone involved would have a satisfactory experience. In this context when I say "those" I'm specifically referring to white people, for too often their unconscious bias causes them to tune out or go on the defensive when a Black person merely suggests that they do something differently. When we're not always in a micro-aggressive situation, we can actually find commonalities.

a lot about the art of Reiki—something he's exploring at the moment.[20]

Still, hair care services can be a frustration for Black women. I prefer to do my own hair; I seldom go to salons. However, it is nice to be pampered and no one likes to pay money for a service only to have to instruct the practitioner on how to carry out that service.

#TeachBlackHairCareAtHairDesignSchools

---

20   In my conversation with him, I saw someone who was thriving, as he told me of his newly developed passion for Reiki. He was excited for his future and told me about a divination he had received—he would move cities and would at some point have three children. I was happy with the end result of the hair service and happy that it led to a beautiful exchange between us.

"I DON'T THINK THERE WILL BE ANYTHING FOR US"

23 JUNE 2014

Even warrior women sometimes have to don / dresses of green silk
/ and put away, for a while at least, their martial garb / Even warrior
women / sometimes have to cease listening to Artemis' songs / and
listen to the silver chants / of the young griot woman in love

—AFUA COOPER, *Copper Woman and Other Poems*

I am back from the boot camp! I had such a phenomenal experience with such phenomenal people. I went by my friend's house to try on my prom dress—her cousin is making it for me.

Oh prom, prom, prom. All the excitement. Honestly, I am not feeling too excited. Let me see how tomorrow pans out. "Uggh, I just hope the music is good," I said to my friend. She sighed, "I don't think there will be anything for us." We were outside standing on her back porch basking in the afternoon sun.

"What do you mean? As in it will be—?"

"—yeah, all white music."

"Hmm . . . I know what you mean."

"I know, and would you think there is only one Black teacher in the whole school," she said. There are over eighty teachers in total at our school. "You know teachers are role models and it's really unfortunate that there is only one Black teacher at the school because when you see someone who looks like you in an influential role, the possibility of you succeeding becomes more real. We mirror our role models.

"People like to categorize themselves into groups with people who are similar to themselves; it is what makes us human. When we fail to see role models like ourselves, we start to become confused. We question and attempt to validate ourselves. When the search to validate ourselves turns sour we start to develop self-hatred. The white students at our school always try to do everything we do, but we can't do everything they do. We are too unique to try to assimilate. We have unique hair and skin. When we look at hair and make-up tutorials online, we always try to find people who look like us. And then there are those people who want to feel and fondle your hair as if it's some creature. Teachers have done that to my hair before—you would think that they'd have more decency."

She also told me about her experience at a predominantly white middle school. She was the only Black student in the whole school. "It was awful. I so wanted to be like them. I wanted be white. It was especially hard because I had just come from Nigeria—where my school was majority Black—and I was only ten years old. They made fun of everything about me, my clothes, my accent. 'Why are you so dark?' they would ask me." That one made me laugh, because relative to me, my friend is light-skinned . . . But I guess it's all *relative*. #Ironic. "I did try to act like them," she continued, "to assimilate. I started wearing lots of short-shorts, tried to do my hair like them—"

"—only to realize that you could never really be like them? Because you were not them."

"Exactly."

"I know what you mean," I said. "I think it's worst when you aspire to emulate someone based on who they are, as in, their physical features and their culture. That's the worst type of emulation, because in the end you'll never succeed. In the case of aspiring to someone's intellect or quality of character, that's different—study hard for the next test and you could get 100 percent. But wanting to have someone's hair or skin colour—you could bleach, but then you risk killing yourself in the process." #SkinCancer

"Wow," she said looking off into the distance at the wilderness ahead. "Thank God that phase is done."

"And this one," I said referring to our completion of high school.

"Next phase," we both said simultaneously.

#HighSchoolAndTheBlackBody

ON THE "FIST PUMP"

25 JUNE 2014
1:12 A.M. WEDNESDAY

Never limit yourself because of others' limited imagination;
never limit others because of your own limited imagination.

—MAE JEMISON

P rom was prom . . . nothing more, nothing less . . . Let
me not seem ungrateful. My friends and I, along with
several family friends took some lovely pictures at the
Public Gardens where all the graduates convened for
about an hour prior to prom.

Now to talk about the "fist pump." Yes, I've promised myself to never do that "dance" on the dance floor.

Fist pump: upon extensive observation and reflection of
the movement(s) of the majority of my peers on the dance
floor tonight, I have come to the conclusion that the "fist
pump" is a lethal "dance." I was unaware that there exists
so many variations of such a mundane movement. Tonight,
I witnessed the downward pump, the upward pump, the in-
ward pump, the outward pump. You see, the thing is, many

people, I realize, pump—which tonight involved a painfully un-rhythmic jump—in a most discordant fashion. #LeapFrog. Now, considering that the dance floor is a shared space (there were about 250 of us on it) your fist pump better be in check. You cannot be leap frogging around the place. It's like control your pump—geesh. Yes, I did receive a minor blow to my shoulder as one young man engaged in the downward pump.

"How was it?" one of the hall staff asked my friend and me at the coat check as we were on our way out.

"You know, the music wasn't as diverse as our school is . . . it was decent," my friend replied.

Yeah, the music didn't reflect the diversity of the student body. I'm not really a huge fan of the word "diversity" these days. I think it's been watered down and that it doesn't truly hit the nail on the head . . . But, it has its uses.

"Will you be going to an after party?" she asked us.

"Oh no. I'll go home and throw my own after party . . . seriously," I said.

ON THE NAME GAME

26 JUNE 2014

Life is full of pain. Let the pain sharpen you,
but don't hold on to it. Don't be bitter.

—TREVOR NOAH, *Born a Crime*

9:40 a.m.

Where: Exhibition Park

What: Graduation Rehearsal

If only she knew how ignorant she sounds.

"We will mispronounce your names. So, you must inform us of the proper pronunciation, if there are any middle names you don't want us to say . . . Halim," she adds, "we will pronounce your name right!" Poor Halim. As my mom would say, "It's only two syllables—shorter than *El-i-za-beth*." And the names drone on.

My internal monologue: *Siguiko ka siguiko ma dey . . . baaraka di sigui ka ta . . .*

When will this end?

GRADUATION *DEH*!
#BEINGAWARRIOR

27 JUNE 2014

Inside of every seed is the DNA of an entire tree, and the blueprint of a forest that will grow out of it. You are a seed. You do not "have" what it takes to fulfill your purpose, you *are* what it takes.

—JORDON VEIRA, Toronto spoken word poet, 1993–2019

Today was the big graduation! It was big, let me tell you: a graduating class of 436 students. The IB graduation was smaller. It was an intimate celebratory event for all of the graduating IB students. Today's graduation was for all of the graduating students regardless of their academic programs.

It was interesting. I am extremely happy to be done this journey. It was too long as far as I'm concerned and too carelessly hurtful. I think I would have been good with two years only.

My friend gave the valedictory address along with another student. Her co-valedictorian talked about what it means to be a "Warrior"—our school icon. Many of her definitions of what it means to be a Warrior did not resonate with me. In her concluding definition, she declared her pride in being from a *diverse* school.

Hmmm, I thought, *I guess for some having diversity on the surface level—student body—is enough. And for them that's okay. But for others, like myself, it is simply not enough.* I am part of that surface level diversity as a Black student, but I am not proud of it because at a deeper level the lack of diversity has been so impactful on my everyday learning experience.

Following the ceremony, I returned to the school with my friend for the reception. My beloved French teacher joined us there. She said to me, "I hope you find happiness wherever you go, because you deserve to be happy . . . I loved how you'd enter the classroom dancing and singing on some mornings. If only you knew what it did for me. You have a happy bird inside you." *How sweet*. She uttered those words at such a timely moment, because today I needed them most. I was having a particularly difficult graduation experience.

My friend and I ended off the reception by saluting some teachers and fellow graduates, and signing their yearbooks . . . My last few moments spent at the school were heartfelt. It seems that throughout the school year so many of my moments were heartfelt but with so much negativity surrounding them. Closure is good indeed. It opens up the way for a New Beginning as I like to say. One that is potentially better than the previous. Of course, that statement is very vague, but I think you have an idea of the kind of New Beginning I'm referring to, based on the content of the previous chapters.

Afterwards, I went and grabbed a bite to eat, then went for a long walk with a few stops and phone calls in between. "Hold on to your core values even when people don't like it. At least you know you've stayed true to yourself," my friend tells me. Another friend, two nights prior: "Overcoming one test is merely a preparation for a bigger one. The first one is meant to strengthen you for the second . . . every step you take today is a graduation from yesterday. It's the journey to the graduation that matters."

#HighSchoolAndTheBlackBody

THE ACADEMIC ELITE[21]

28 JUNE 2014

> The forces that unite us are intrinsic and greater than
> the superimposed influences that keep us apart.
> —KWAME NKRUMAH, *Africa Must Unite*

began the International Baccalaureate (IB) program in the seventh grade when I began Middle Years Program (MYP) at my middle school in Toronto. I *loved* middle school. My school was small—a student population of about two hundred. I appreciated that, for it meant students were given great opportunities to bond with teachers and receive individualized feedback. While there were niches among the students, the smallness of our social and learning spaces meant that at some point the various niches had to interact. We were a tight-knit community.

I remember that, when leaving the sixth grade, I begged my mother to not enrol me in the Extended French program

---

21 What I would have said, if they'd asked me to give the IB Graduation Address. I believe this is another example of my constant experience of racism making me more aware at a young age of all kinds of inequity.

that was being offered at my then-prospective junior high. I asked my father to intervene and advocate on my behalf. It was all to no avail. I was not expressly against the Extended French program. I've always loved language, and I had excelled during the brief exposure I had to French in elementary school. However, there was a particular someone who would not be enrolling in Extended French; hence, I deemed it unnecessary for me to do so . . . To this day, I thank my mother for insisting that I do the program.

Upon walking into school that first morning of the eighth grade, I was elated to find that my homeroom teacher was a Black woman. She was new to my peers and myself. We would have her for all of our classes that were taught in French: History, Geography, and French language. She was not at the school the year prior when we were in Grade 7. I remember her insisting that we all form a line and walk up the stairs uniformly to our classroom. She came off as "no-nonsense" to the group, but we quickly grew to love her. I went home that day beaming. "Mom, my teacher is Black!" I announced excitedly. She is the third Black teacher who has ever taught me and the third woman of colour to teach me in my entire educational career. She went above and beyond her call of duty as a teacher, greatly accelerating our learning as she taught us several French language tenses that were not on the curriculum for her to cover with us that year. It was an asset to us because we entered high school French with a very strong foundation.

I had a most wonderful middle school experience. I was introduced to the core philosophies of the IB program and the IB Areas of Interaction, which include Community and Service, Health and Social Education, Environments, Approaches to Learning, and Human Ingenuity. The teachers ensured that every assignment we did related to one of the Areas of Interaction and it was incumbent upon us as students to identify and explain the ways in which our assignments connected to each area. For example, we had to connect a Grade 7 science research project we did on acid rain to the area of Environments, and discuss the environmental impacts of acid rain.

The teachers delivered the curriculum in a way that was relevant to the lives of the students. #TenetNo1OfTeaching Also, in Grade 7 we had to do a Human Ingenuity project during which all of the students were arranged into small groups that had to develop plans to solve pressing social and environmental issues. At the end, all of the groups presented their innovations at a school-wide assembly. Projects ranged from a coffee filter prototype that could be further developed to use in the clean-up of ocean oil spills, to a student association that would engage in resource sharing by offering school supplies to students who were without. #InnovativeSchooling

One of my favourite aspects of my middle school experience was the IB Learner Profile announcements. Every morning two students—I did it on several occasions— would announce an IB learner characteristic followed by a definition of that characteristic over the intercom. The characteristic of the day might have been "open-minded," "principled," "reflective," or "caring"—attributes that should be embodied by IB students. As I began the IB Diploma program in high school, I realized that all of that had gone with the wind.

At my eighth grade graduation I felt refreshed, invigorated, and I was looking forward to a New Beginning. Nostalgia did set in, but it was a pleasant nostalgia; nostalgia evocative of the extent to which I would miss my teachers and the comfort of the learning environment they created for the students.

Throughout high school, I was skeptical whether students and some teachers were even aware of what the IB Learner Profile and Areas of Interaction are. At least, even if certain teachers were, it surely did not seem to seep into their teaching. #Disappointed. Education is more than a 100 percent on your transcript. Education is to make students worldlier, and to broaden their horizons.

Perhaps my biggest pet peeve about the IB ethos I witnessed in high school is . . . *du-dum* . . . The Academic Elite. Several of my IB peers referred to themselves as the Academic Elite within our school. A few teachers have also said that: "You guys are the Academic Elite; we expect more from you." I feel that such "elitism" naturally creates divisions between IB students and non-IB students (those who are in other academic streams). The paradox is that the school in its entirety aims to foster a sense of cohesion among all students, yet there is no doubt that many students, teachers, and administrative staff believe that IB students are superior to the rest. Such thinking only helps to foster a sense of disunion among students.

Often when I told people—my own friends included—that I was in IB they responded with an amazed "You're in IB?!"

For some reason there is this notion that only a select few students are suitable for IB. Of course, coming from Toronto where my entire middle school was IB MYP, I find that ridiculous. Any student upon matriculating to my middle school became an IB MYP student. There were no academic divisions, but most importantly, the notion that only certain students are capable of the social and academic requirements of the program was non-existent.

The high school I attended in the tenth grade was a completely IB school. Once again, the notion of an Academic Elite was non-existent.

I graduate from Grade 12 feeling fatigued, relieved, and anticipating a New Beginning . . . minus the nostalgia.

#ReliefFromTheElite

SOCIAL ENTREPRENEURSHIP AND BLACK YOUTH

30 JUNE 2014

When you're in your lane, there's no traffic.

—AVA DUVERNAY, filmmaker

#Innovation #ForcedUponUs #Hope

In recent years, there has been explosive growth in what is known as "Social Entrepreneurship." As defined by Nobel Laureate Muhammad Yunus, Social Entrepreneurship is any innovative initiative that helps people; it can be for-profit or not-for-profit. Boot camps, incubators, and accelerators for Social Entrepreneurship have sprung up everywhere.

In today's Social Entrepreneurship industry, innovation is the keyword. Innovation is the secret to social entrepreneurial success. Innovation could be an idea, a change in perspective, a unique system model, a product, etc. An important characteristic of this #AgeOfInnovation is that it is largely youth-led. As a result, it is forcing us to rethink conventional practices around qualification acquisition (post-secondary certifications from colleges and universities) and entry into the job market. As evidenced by the likes of Mark Zuckerberg, George Foreman, David Karp, Richard Branson, and Simon Cowell, high school is not quintessential to post-secondary success.

Nonetheless, Social Entrepreneurship has a long-standing history among Black youth. For us, Social Entrepreneurship was born out of a need for survival given the social, political, and most importantly economic barriers that have been imposed upon us as a result of living in anti-Black diasporic societies. For many Black youth living in urban cities across North America—Toronto, Vancouver, Halifax, Montreal, Chicago, New York, etc.—entry into the world of Social Entrepreneurship stems from our exit from high school. In an education system that does not want Black students, that inundates our brains with racist curricula, that polices our bodies on a daily basis #Habiba'sIllegalUseOfTheElevator, and whose ethnocentric culture taints our psychosocial experience in high school, dropping out would seem inevitable; and, for many Black students, it is the inevitable result. Once we are out of high school, we are forced to innovate. We must come up with an alternative route to success.

Like I mentioned in an earlier entry, we are made to believe that high school is indispensable to our success in the future. It is what will take us to university, and university in turn will increase our prospects of having a lucrative and respectable career. The massive success experienced by several high school dropouts with Social Entrepreneurship contradicts this notion. For Black high school dropouts, Social Entrepreneurship might mean becoming an amateur hip-hop rap artist, a dancer, or spoken word artist.

I am going to use business terminology in order to discuss how each of these entrepreneurs must use innovation to improve their economic condition. Say, for example, each of the entrepreneurs begins business as a "start-up," meaning that they do not have any initial external capital to finance the business. The rap artist must find free studio space to record his records; the dancer must seek opportunities to perform at nightclubs and s/he hopes for cash in return; the spoken word artist hopes to make a name for herself through "poetry slams" and be paid honorariums at future events. In this context, the entrepreneurs' initial "investment" in the business is understood to be the time, energy, and effort they must expend to access free resources to begin operations. Note that there is no capital or monetary investment. They simply cannot afford to finance their businesses with capital. Moreover, given their age and socio-economic background, they do not have any credit history and would not qualify for a bank loan to finance the business. Their "return on investment" is thus the cash they receive for their work. For the rap artist this would mean CD sales; for the dancer, income from nightclub performances; for the spoken word artist, payments from literary events and poetry slams. What is the social impact for each of the entrepreneurs? Survival. These initiatives are a testament to how Black youth channel their human ingenuity into innovative ventures in order to improve their economic standing. This innovation is born out of a need to improve our condition as human beings.

In our current Social Entrepreneurship climate, innovation is often associated with technology-related ventures, for example, with the development of mobile/web apps and social media networks like Tumblr and Facebook. Furthermore, it seems to be that an underlying assumption of Social Entrepreneurship is that the social entrepreneur engages in business that creates social impact for another, less fortunate group of people—people other than the entrepreneur herself. However, in the context of the Black youth I am discussing in this entry, Social Entrepreneurship—for all intents and purposes—is pursued for the purpose of creating social impact for the entrepreneur herself. I have explained the reasons for which many Black students drop out: push factors like the racism and policing that we are subjected to in schools. We, therefore, use our human ingenuity as leverage to enter into the world of Social Entrepreneurship to improve our economic condition, which—due to dropping out of school—becomes compromised, as opportunities to become trade workers or professionals are hindered as a result of not having a high school diploma. Black youth take this hopeless situation and turn it into something productive in spite of racial barriers that are inherent in the process.

Can this kind of Social Entrepreneurship be supported in the same way as conventional Social Entrepreneurship? Basically, can incubators and accelerators give the hip-hop artist start-up funding, networking support, and mentorship from people in like industries to drive innovation that will support his life? Can he become part of entrepreneurial spaces like hubs and boot camps that will offer him the same opportunity to access funding as someone of a higher socio-economic status and someone who is eligible for a bank loan? This type of support would ultimately allow him to take his innovation from the streets into the marketplace.

I believe that this unique kind of Social Entrepreneurship pursued by Black youth in diasporic communities across the Western world is the greatest kind of innovation because it is forced upon us for our survival.

#LEGACIES

18 JULY 2014

In every human Breast, God has implanted a
Principle, which we call Love of Freedom; it is impatient
of Oppression, and pants for Deliverance.

—PHILLIS WHEATLEY

I am attending an Underground Railroad conference in Detroit with my mother. Last night we saw a theatrical representation of a slave narrative by Washington Productions Inc. They enacted the story of the Conner family, who, in 1849, travelled north in order to avoid being captured into southern slavery. Whenever I hear of, or watch films or plays about, slave narratives my body gets cold; a chill runs down my back. The slaves come to life and I, as the spectator, a spectator who has a particular connection to their lives, begin to have a physiological reconnaissance of their experience.

The Conner family were freed people who made the decision to travel north to Canada given their vulnerable, albeit freed, condition. Many freed slaves and Blacks who were born free were often deceived and re-captured into slavery. The recent film *12 Years a Slave* chronicles the life of Solomon Northup who is an example of that. As the Conners crossed the colossal Blue Ridge Mountains, they were stopped several times by slave patrollers—men who travelled around searching for runaway slaves in order to return them to their "masters."

The first time they were stopped, the family was interrogated, but on presenting their free papers were allowed to go on. The next time they were stopped, Auntie Rosie's papers were nowhere to be found. Frantically, she and her family searched their wagon and all of their belongings for the papers. *Rien* . . . She appealed to the patrollers. Told them that if she could go back to where they had been previously she would surely find the papers. She was hauled into the patrollers' wagon, a "free" woman, captured into slavery. The Conner family continued north without her. Aunt Rosie was never heard from again.

What did happen to her free papers? When William Conner presented the family's papers to the first group of patrollers, they did not give them all back. The Conners were deceived.

After the presentation, I said to a friend, "It was very powerful. The patrollers' theft of Auntie Rosie's free papers, and the mere fact that they had to uproot themselves as 'free' people in order to gain real 'freedom' in the north, really underscored the vulnerability of their situation." Their story reminded me of Africville, a former Black community within the city of Halifax that was wantonly destroyed by municipal authorities in the early 1960s. I wrote a paper on the dismantling of Africville for a history research project. I found the research process riveting. I consulted films like *Remember Africville* and listened to former Africville residents speak first-hand about how the dismantling of their homes and the relocation process that followed killed them spiritually and psychologically.

I remember once, in the tenth grade, my English class watched a film on slave narratives called *Unchained Memories No Lies*. I was away the day the students viewed it, so I watched it separately in an unoccupied classroom when I returned. When I was finished watching the film, the teacher who was facilitating the screening for me walked in to take the DVD player back to the tech room. "How was it?" she asked me.

"Wow," I said, "I get chills whenever I watch these films."

"I can only imagine that *you* would."

"Yeah . . ." was all I could say.

It occurred to me then that she did not have the same experience and could not wholly understand my relationship to the film. *She should get chills too*, I thought to myself. *But why would she? This did not happen to her people. She does not have the same historical or bodily connection. Slavery brutalized the bodies of Black people. Bodies like my own. Whites were perpetrators in the industry of slavery, not victims. They do not carry the psychic and physical burden of slavery.*

It makes me question the extent to which Black people have gained physical liberty—the right to express, present, and portray our bodies as we see fit. #PhysicalAutonomy. On what levels have we gained physical liberty? It is true that Black bodies are no longer subject to the whips of bondage as they were during plantation slavery in the Americas. Nevertheless, whenever I see commercials by charitable organizations—those that exploit images of young children purportedly from Ethiopia or Mali walking three miles to get water with flies on their faces as a strategy to capitalize on donor spending from guilt-ridden child sponsors, while they pay themselves large sums in administrative overhead fees—I am reminded that our physical autonomy as Black people is compromised and that it is at the disposal of "well-intentioned" white people.

I always relate these past experiences of Black people to my own experience as a Black student in high school, and I ask myself: *Given these legacies of unrelenting racism and hatred towards Blacks, can white teachers and administrators be truly anti-racist? And if so, what are the requirements?* One cannot ignore the fact that the vast majority of these white staff—Baby Boomers—grew up during an era of heightened racial tension, and anti-Black racism: lynchings, segregated schools, etc. The households in which they were brought up would have been headed by parents who—given the social, political, and ideological climate of the time—viewed Blacks as an inferior race. I do not mean to generalize, for I know that there is the rare individual with an anti-racist consciousness who grew up during that era. Nonetheless, racism is a systemic phenomenon; thus, the ideologies of this Baby Boomer class of white teachers must be assessed systemically. One could argue that with the "changing" of times (for example an end to lynchings and segregated schools) that the ideologies of white teachers who grew up during the era have also changed. I beg to differ. Considering the pervasiveness of whitewashing and the racism that pervades media, advertising, education, and social culture, I would argue that deep psychological intervention is necessary for white individuals to have a paradigm shift with respect to how they view Black people.

The insidiousness of this kind of mental racism embedded in the high school environment for Black students like me is that we are having to continually challenge every experience, ask ourselves why something makes us so angry, so uncomfortable, because our teachers are the representatives of institutionalized racism. #Africa #EquatorPeople #ThatEnglishClassWasF*cked #MsPinkSweater #AWalkFor Water #FoodForThought

#MIKEBROWN #FERGUSON #HALIFAX

19 AUGUST 2014

Violence has no jurisdiction,
neither does solidarity.

—AGNES OLOWOGBOYE, third-year law student

Today, three of my friends held a six-hundred-person strong rally in support of Michael Brown, an unarmed, eighteen-year-old Black male from Ferguson, Missouri, who was fatally shot by a white police officer last week, on August 9, 2014. The officer approached Brown and his friend who were walking on the street, and demanded that they walk on the sidewalk. Soon after, Brown received fatal shots all over his body.

#IfTheyGunnedMeDown #JusticeForMikeBrown #Justice ForBounaAndZyed #StopPoliceBrutality

Ntombi, one of the rally organizers (left), and I at the rally. Photo courtesy of the author.

CONCLUSION

I AM DONE *DEH*!
30 AUGUST 2014

My challenge to each of you is that you ask yourself
what you can do to make a difference. And then take that
action, no matter how large or how small.

—GRAÇA MACHEL

Our education system does not benefit Black students. It does not help us self-actualize. On the contrary, it is often an impediment to our self-actualization, and a denial of our potential. When people see the phrase Black Body they conjure up all sorts of racist and unpalatable stereotypes and rhetoric about Black people. The fact that that is the first place dominant culture's imagination goes when thinking of Black bodies compromises our self-worth and puts us in a constant state of combat, fighting to reassert our humanity.

High school is not merely a slew of ideologies etched into textbooks. It is a deeply soulful experience, one that requires the Black student to continually self-reflect on who she is and where her identity rests in an environment that invalidates her practices and her cultural values; in an institution where her life experiences are perpetually portrayed as primitive, backward, hypersexual, and inferior; where her mere existence is a challenge to the physical spaces like hallways and classrooms that she may occupy throughout the day; and where her humanity is perpetually under critical examination but through a superficial and selective lens.

Nonetheless, my time spent in high school was bittersweet. Over the four years, I had some of the most amazing opportunities to study abroad and participate in science camps, academic summer programs, and leadership summits, all while forming friendships with very talented, warm-spirited individuals. Many of those opportunities stemmed from my founding of a non-profit organization called the Women's Health Organization International (WHOI), which I established in Grade 10 to put an end to a maternal health condition called obstetric fistula. But the context in which those great and sweet experiences occurred need not have been so bitter.

How do we, then, put an end to this cycle of racism towards Black students, so that the bodies of the future generations of Black students will not be hurt, stigmatized, hindered, and nullified in high school?

I leave the Black students reading this book with a challenge: to ensure that you make your voices heard, that you do not compromise your personal and cultural values for the happiness of someone else or of an institution. You might argue that taking a stand against systemic, institutionalized racism requires too much energy and effort, effort that you would rather channel into achieving a 4.0 GPA. But ask yourself this: at what cost to your mental and emotional health will you attain that 4.0?

And I leave the white and white-influenced educators with this challenge: It is critical that educators, administrators, curriculum consultants, and policy makers design programs that are reflective of the experiences of Blacks in Canada. This could mean integrating texts such as Sharon G. Flake's *The Skin I'm In* and *Unbowed: A Memoir* by Nobel Laureate Wangari Maathai into the curriculum, having students listen to Isaac Saney or bell hooks at school assemblies (not limited to Black History Month), and assigning work on Imhotep's contributions to philosophy, medicine, and mathematics and Hatshepsut's various expeditions to Punt and Byblos. The experiences of Blacks should be normalized to the same extent as those of Whites. A solely white and Eurocentric approach to education can no longer be sustained if we are to ensure the success and academic excellence of Black (and all) students (because white and Eurocentric students who come out of school without their prejudice and ignorance challenged have been equally failed by the system). The Eurocentric approach to education reinforces ideas of white supremacy and promotes the marginalization of the Black Body.

Is there such a thing as academic responsibility when one's human rights are violated? Several articles of the Universal Declaration of Human Rights are relevant to the analysis of the impact of high school on the Black Body. Articles 1 and 3 affirm the equality and the security of person granted all human beings.[22] However, in high school, equality and security of person is rescinded for Black students. Section 7 of the Canadian Charter of Rights and Freedoms extends Article 3 of the declaration to protect "both the physical and psychological integrity of the individual."[23] Article 22 of the declaration defends every individual's "right to social security," and his or her entitlement to the realization of "social and cultural rights indispensable for his [or her] dignity and the free development of his [or her] personality." Finally, Clause 3 of Article 26 maintains that "parents have a prior right to choose the kind of education that shall be given to their children." Hence, there is the need for parents of Black students to exercise their political power and agitate for the realization of these rights in the educational system. In what other ways can we exercise these rights in light of the multifaceted erosion of the humanity of Black students and the repression of our bodies? The answer might lie in the filing of a class action lawsuit to disclose and also generate concern for the injustices to Black students on a national and legal level.

{I am pleased that in 2018, Prime Minister Justin Trudeau acknowledged anti-Black racism and unconscious bias in Canada because it is time to do so and Black Canadians are citizens too. Though what I would like to see is the anti-Black racism, of which Prime Minister Trudeau speaks, being addressed at the level of primary and secondary education in

22 United Nations, "Universal Declaration of Human Rights," 1948, http://www.un.org/en/documents/udhr/index.shtml.

23 Graham Garton, "Section 7: Life, Liberty and Security of Person," *The Canadian Charter of Rights Decisions Digest, Justice Canada.* (2004), http://canlii.ca/en/commentary/charterDigest/s-7.html.

Canada. Education is transformative and the power to change society lies within it.}

Well, I guess I can stop writing now. I'm done high school. This Black body—spiritual, intellectual, physical, and emotional—is out of it! Let me take a minute to rejoice now . . . *Saludooo!* University, I'm coming with a bang.

In his speech at the founding of the

Habiba in the spring of her first year of university. Photo courtesy of the author.

Organization of Afro-American Unity in 1964, Malcolm X said that we need to declare our rights to be respected as human beings on this earth and claim the rights of human beings in society "by any means necessary."

We need to remember that, for far too long, high school has hurt the Black Body; it is high time not only to struggle against this phenomenon, but also to abolish it once and for all. This is no wishful thinking. This is willful thinking.

For she who hope,

Tell the journey has begun![24]

---

24   Cara Rautins and A. Ibrahim, "Wide-Awakeness: Toward a Critical Pedagogy of Imagination, Humanism and Becoming," *International Journal of Critical Pedagogy* 3, no. 2 (2011): 24–36.

HABIBA COOPER DIALLO was a finalist in the 2020 Bristol Short Story Prize, as well as the 2019 Writers' Union of Canada Short Prose Competition and the 2018 London Book Fair Pitch Competition. She was "highly commended" for the 2018 Manchester Fiction Prize. She is a women's health advocate, who has been building awareness about a maternal health injury, obstetric fistula, since the age of twelve. She self-published her first book, *Yeshialem Learns about Fistula*, in 2015 and is pursuing a master's degree in public health. Habiba lives in Halifax, Nova Scotia. You can find her on Twitter @haalabeeba.